Favorite
Bread Machine
Recipes

▼

Norman A. Garrett

Sterling Publishing Co., Inc. New York

Acknowledgments

Without the assistance and encouragement of many people, this present book wouldn't have been possible. I'd like to thank readers of my first two books for their letters and comments, all of which encouraged me to continue with my third book.

I thank my wife, Margie, and my children, Rachel, Ethan, Josh, Aaron, and Emily, for their help, patience, and encouragement as I developed new recipes.

I'd also like to thank the staff of Sterling Publishing Co., Inc., for their faith in this project and for their attention to detail.

Library of Congress Cataloging-in-Publication Data

Garrett, Norman A.
    Favorite bread machine recipes / by Norman A. Garrett.
        p.   cm.
    Includes index.
    ISBN 0-8069-0540-9 (pbk.)
    1. Bread.   2. Automatic bread machines.   I. Title.
TX769.G36   1994   93-47247
641.8'15—dc20   CIP

10 9 8 7 6 5 4 3 2

Published by Sterling Publishing Company, Inc.
387 Park Avenue South, New York, N.Y. 10016
© 1994 by Norman A. Garrett
Distributed in Canada by Sterling Publishing
% Canadian Manda Group, P.O. Box 920, Station U
Toronto, Ontario, Canada M8Z 5P9
Distributed in Great Britain and Europe by Cassell PLC
Villiers House, 41/47 Strand, London WC2N 5JE, England
Distributed in Australia by Capricorn Link (Australia) Pty Ltd.
P.O. Box 6651, Baulkham Hills, Business Centre, NSW 2153, Australia
Manufactured in the United States of America
All rights reserved

Sterling ISBN 0-8069-0540-9 (Paper)

CONTENTS

INTRODUCTION

My first two books, *Great Bread Machine Recipes* and *Quick & Delicious Bread Machine Recipes*, received such excellent responses that I continued to develop new recipes. My goal was to develop bread-machine recipes that would be original, healthful, tasty, and fun to prepare. The result is this third book.

All of the recipes in this book are original creations, with ideas drawn from various sources, including family recipe files, friends and associates, and even cereal boxes. Since standard bread recipes vary greatly, all must undergo a conversion process in order to work in a bread machine.

Each recipe in this book has undergone a rigorous process of conversion and experimentation. Here's how to convert your favorite bread recipes so that you can use them with your bread machine.

After I began to experiment with my bread machine, I began to record (for future reference) the good recipes and make notes on the failures. Once I mastered the machine's operation, I wrote some computer software to help me to develop recipes. The software helped me experiment with fewer failures, and I began to formulate a set of guidelines for bread-machine recipes that, when adhered to, would usually yield good results.

The recipes in this book vary greatly and use different types of grains, flours, seeds, and other ingredients. Baking different kinds of bread is an exciting and tantalizing activity. Baking your own bread gives you total control over what you eat. In this era of heightened health consciousness, knowing what you eat is very important.

The breads in this book contain only natural ingredients, so you can select recipes that not only appeal to your palate but also give you a nutritional boost. Diets need not eliminate bread, as long as the bread is wholesome, with few empty calories. To help you evaluate the recipes, I calculated the nutritional values for each of the breads in this book.

There are many bread machines on the market, but not all will bake bread the same. The machines vary in motor size, baking capacity, cycle types and lengths, baking options, and appearance. When I tested recipes in various machines, I found considerable variation in the quality of the bread they produced. All of the recipes in this book were tested in Hitachi machines, and I tried to adjust the recipes to work in most other machines. However, where modifications might be necessary, they will be indicated in the recipes. Be sure to read the notes for each recipe to get the best results from your machine.

Feel free to experiment. Experimentation allowed me to develop the recipes in this book. Once you become familiar with bread's ingredients, you'll be able to make substitutions, convert standard bread recipes, and even produce your own creations. Many of the breads in this book were derived from standard recipes, and they evolved through experimentation into original creations that work well in a bread machine.

Consider these recipes as a beginning, and make notes in the margins of this book. Watch the machine work. Become familiar with its sounds, its cycles, and the texture of the doughs it produces. One you're familiar with your machine, you'll want to strike out on your own to try new and wonderful breads. Happy baking!

GETTING TO KNOW YOUR BREAD MAKER

Basic Operation

Although bread machines come in various shapes, sizes, and capacities, they all share certain characteristics and principles of operation. They are all designed to make bread making quick and easy. Other than your placing the proper ingredients in the baking pan, pressing a few buttons, and removing the bread when it is finished (and slicing it, of course), the machine does all the work.

After you place the ingredients in the pan and start the machine, the following cycles occur:

1. Initial mix
2. First rise
3. "Punch down"
4. Second rise
5. Bake
6. Cool-down

The length of each cycle will depend on the make and model of your machine. Some machines skip the second rise and they bake after the first rise. Other machines have alternate settings that let you select a double or single rise (often called the "quick-bread" cycle). Some of the newer machines have cycles especially created for whole-grain breads, which generally require longer rising cycles. In addition, some machines have special cycles for cooking rice, jam, quick breads (batter breads), and cakes.

Whatever machine you use, become familiar with the way it works, so that you can tap its full potential.

Capacities

Each machine has a maximum capacity. Capacities are usually either one pound or 1½ pounds, although a few machines accommodate 2-pound loaves. Don't exceed the rated capacity of your machine, because overloading can cause dough overflows or motor damage.

I have seen machines that claim to bake "three-pound loaves," but usually these machines will only produce a dense bread that doesn't rise much. Don't bake loaves much larger than what your machine can handle because of the strain an overload places on the motor.

Can you bake a loaf that's smaller than the rated capacity? With most machines, there will be no problem. The recipes in this book are presented in both

1-pound and 1½-pound sizes. If you have a 1-pound machine, limit yourself to baking 1-pound loaves. If you have a larger, 1½-pound machine, try both recipe sizes.

Table 1 shows the basic capacities of bread machines currently on the market. Determine he capacity of your machine by reading the owner's manual and by checking the white-bread recipe included in the manual. If the recipe calls for two cups of bread flour, you have a 1-pound machine. If it calls for three or more cups, you have a 1½-pound (or greater) capacity machine.

Table 1—Bread Machine Capacities

Flour Amount (Basic White Bread (Recipe)	1 Pound	1½ Pound	1½ + Pound
2 cups	X		
2.5	X		
3		X	
3.5			X
3–4			X

Note: Determine the amount of flour called for in the basic white-bread recipe for your machine. This chart will tell you the capacity of your machine based on that amount. If you do not have access to the basic white-bread recipe that came with your machine, assume that it has a 1-pound capacity.

Baking the Dough Yourself

All bread machines let you bake the dough yourself. Simply extract the dough from the machine after the first rise is complete. If your machine has a dough setting, the machine will beep when it is time to remove the dough. You can then punch the dough down, knead it, and place it in bread pans or on cookie sheets for a final rise and baking.

Adding Ingredients

Some machines have a mix-bread setting, which will beep when it is time to add raisins, seeds, or other ingredients to the dough. Since not all machines have this cycle, the recipes in this book have been written so that all ingredients can be placed in the pan at the beginning. However, if you have a mix cycle, you can use that cycle, particularly with the recipes calling for seeds, nuts, or raisins. The advantage to adding these ingredients during a mix cycle is that they receive less pounding during the mixing process. Raisins, for example, will usually remain whole when the mix-bread setting is used.

Crusts

Most machines allow you to select the darkness of the crust. The timing for the crust will usually determine the baking temperature of your bread, but it won't alter the length of the baking cycle, which varies from machine to machine. Setting the control for a darker crust will increase the temperature of the oven. Turning the dial (on one model) to the lightest crust setting caused some breads to have uncooked dough in the middle. It will probably take a few loaves for you to determine the best setting to accommodate both your machine's capabilities and your personal taste. Once you determine that setting, make note of it, because you'll probably want to bake all of your loaves on that same setting.

Knowing Your Own Machine

Get used to your particular machine. When testing recipes for my books, I found considerable variations among different machines. Familiarize yourself with two parts of the baking process as they apply to your specific machine: the optimum consistency of your dough, and the way your machine sounds as it goes through the various cycles.

Dough Consistency

Dough consistency and each machine's ability to deal with different dough consistencies are important and vary widely. Some machines work best with a runny dough (more liquid content), while others have powerful motors that can easily handle stiffer doughs. Observe your bread as it mixes, making a mental note of the dough consistency. Then, when the bread is done, note its texture. Learn to correlate the finished texture with the consistency of the dough. Soon you will be able to accurately predict the texture of the bread by looking at the dough immediately after mixing. This skill is important if you want to make any recipe modifications.

Machine Sounds

As you use your machine, also note the sounds it makes as it goes through its various cycles. Once you become familiar with the normal sounds, you will be aware when the motor is making unusual noises, indicating that the motor is being overworked, which can damage the machine.

Service & Cleaning

Cleaning

If you want consistently good bread, make sure your machine is clean. Taking two to three minutes after each loaf has baked to clean the machine will yield consistently good loaves and assure that your machine remains in peak operating condition.

The difficulty in cleaning the machines varies according to their design. Some machines use a bucket with the beater drive mechanism built in. Consequently, cleaning is simply a matter of removing the bread from the bucket, removing the beater, and cleaning the bucket with warm water. On other machines, the beater-drive mechanism is not part of the bucket, and the former must be cleaned after each use. Cleaning such machines is more difficult, and "debris" sometimes results in crumbs in the bottom of the baking chamber.

A damp kitchen washcloth will pick up most crumbs from the baking chambers. I have tried mini-vacuums, canned air, and other methods, such as turning the whole unit upside down and shaking it, but find that using a washcloth works the best (and is the least messy).

The bread pan on all machines has a special, nonstick surface that requires care. Don't use any abrasive cleaners or scouring pads on the inside of the bread pan, or you'll damage the nonstick surface. Try not to pry out stuck bread by using knives, forks, or other hard objects that may scratch the pan's surface. If you must pry, use a rubber (or soft plastic) device of some kind (such as a rubber spatula). If you take proper care of your bread pan, it will yield many loaves of bread.

The machines with the beater mechanism as part of the housing (rather than as part of the bread bucket) also have a small plastic washer. Be careful with this washer. Don't lose it. Remember to rinse it off and dry it after making each loaf of bread. Without the washer, you won't have a good seal between the bucket and the bottom of the baking chamber, and leakage will occur.

If you have an accident with your bread machine (overflow or other big mess), wait until it cools down and then take your time cleaning it. Most baked-on bread can be removed with warm water, and that is the recommended means of cleanup. I've had my share of disasters, but I have managed to clean all of them up without even using any soap. Just warm water and a washcloth have always been all that was needed.

Lost & Damaged Parts

There are generally no user-serviceable components in the bread machine, other than those just mentioned. However, there are parts that are easily lost or damaged, which you can replace yourself. Most prominent on the list is the mixer beater. Since it is a small, removable part, it is easily misplaced. Replace the beater in the bucket after each cleaning so you won't lose it.

On machines with a plastic washer beneath the bread bucket, the washer will wear out after a while. If your machine has one of these, in addition to keeping it clean, it would be a good idea to order a replacement to have on hand. This washer is inexpensive.

The Bread Pan

The other major removable component is the bread pan itself. Probably the most likely damage is to its nonstick surface. If the surface becomes damaged to the point where bread sticks to it, replace the bread pan. As long as you're able to remove the bread from the pan, don't be concerned about small scratches.

Major Repairs

If any other problems arise with your machine, you'll probably have to send it out for repair. The control panel, for example, will sometimes cease to function and will need to be replaced. Obtain an estimate before authorizing any major repairs on your machine, because it's possible that the cost of the repairs will exceed the cost of the machine. The likelihood is that your machine will have a long, productive life, and that it will give you many hours of trouble-free bread baking, if you simply keep it clean and ready for the next loaf.

Troubleshooting Guide

There are many variables that can affect your bread. Those discussed below are all problems I have experienced myself while making bread in my bread machine. You may also encounter some not listed here. Before you abandon your bread machine completely or send it out for repair, think the problem through and make sure that you've accounted for all the possible reasons for the problem. These could include wrong crust setting, improper baking cycle, measuring ingredients improperly, using stale ingredients, failure to check for power outages during baking (which may recycle your machine), and, finally, curious children pushing buttons.

Stuck Dough Beater

If the dough beater is difficult to remove after baking a loaf of bread, use some shortening on the shaft before installing the beater and place dry ingredients in the pan first. With a machine whose beater is self-contained in the pan, soak the beater in water for a few minutes after removing the bread. In some machines, the beater will stay with the loaf of bread and is rarely a problem to remove.

Liquid Leakage

This might be a problem with machines whose pans have a hole in the bottom to accommodate the dough beater. With these machines, dry ingredients should be placed in the bread pan first and liquids added last. Also, check to make sure you have the rubber sealing washer in the proper position before locking the pan in place. Then make sure that the pan is securely locked before adding the ingredients.

Recipe Failure

To avoid a failure, make sure you use the ingredients in their proper quantities. It's easy to become distracted while setting up a recipe and to miscount the ingredients. Also, make sure you choose the correct settings for baking the bread. In addition, be sure to use the proper ingredients and that they are fresh.

Loaf-Size Variation

While the weight of two loaves of bread may be the same, their size and appearance may vary greatly. This is due to the different ingredients used. In general, breads using gluten-rich bread flour will rise more than will breads using flours with less gluten content. Rye breads, for example, will be small, with a dense texture and a darker crust. The loaf sizes of the recipes in this book refer to weight, not to finished size.

Spoiled Ingredients

The two ingredients with which you must be especially cautious are fresh eggs and fresh milk. Do not use either of them in a delay-bake cycle (available on some machines), where you set the timer to start the bread at a later time. Use milk if the delay is not more than an hour or two, but don't use eggs in any recipe that won't be started immediately. If you want to use a recipe calling for eggs on a delay bake, consider using powdered eggs instead of fresh eggs. If you want to use milk in a delayed recipe, use dry milk and add the proper amount of water.

Collapsing Dough

In this case, the dough probably rose for too long a period. Since the timer cycles are not programmable on most machines, consider reducing the yeast by ½ teaspoon to get less rising. Check to make sure that the machine was not recycled during the process. Recycling can occur from brief power outages or children (or curious adults) pressing machine buttons. If you become aware that a power outage has occurred, you can remove the dough from the machine and finish the process by hand, baking the bread in the oven.

Strong Yeast Flavor

Here, it is possible that too much yeast was added. Cut the yeast down by ½ teaspoon and try again.

Failure to Rise

This can be a complex problem with many possible causes. Any of the following will inhibit rising:

- Using flour with low-gluten content (pure rye flour, wheat flour, etc.).
- Too much salt in the recipe. Salt is a yeast inhibitor.
- Too little sugar in the recipe. Sugar feeds yeast and promotes rising.
- Old yeast. Check the yeast supply and make sure to use fresh yeast. Old yeast won't activate and rise properly.
- Dead yeast. This may be caused by adding hot ingredients. For example, if your recipe calls for some ingredients to be boiled before being added to the mix, don't add them until they have had time to cool. Adding ingredients that are too hot will kill yeast.

Uneven Top

This usually indicates too little liquid in the recipe. However, with some breads, such as rye breads, where less rising takes place, this may be a normal occurrence.

Collapsed Top

This is usually caused by too much liquid in the recipe. Cut the liquid back by two tablespoons and try again. Be careful not to make your bread too stiff, because some machines have underpowered motors that won't be able to handle stiffer dough, particularly with the 1½-pound recipes. Also, be aware that some recipes use ingredients that will add liquid to the dough during the baking cycle, and a collapsed top might be normal. I found this to be the case with breads using fresh cheeses.

Rancid Taste

Check the whole-grain ingredients. Whole-grain flours, wheat germ, and similar ingredients should be kept in the refrigerator or freezer. They spoil rapidly when left at room temperature, and spoiled ingredients will give your bread a rancid taste. White flours, on the other hand, are not subject to the same type of spoilage and can be left in the cupboard at room temperature for storage.

White Spots

White spots occur when flour sticks to the sides of the pan during the mixing process and isn't mixed into the dough. When the bread rises and bakes, this flour sticks to the outside of the loaf. While not posing a problem of taste, it can present a cosmetic one. Look into the baking pan after the mixing has taken place, and, if there's flour stuck to the sides of the pan, take a rubber spatula and remove it and mix it in with the dough.

Soggy Crust

Your bread will have a soggy crust if you leave it in the pan too long after the baking cycle is finished. Some machines have cooling cycles that will cool the bread and remove the moisture. A soggy crust is not as great a problem with these machines, but it's still a good idea to remove the bread and place it on a cooling rack after the final beep.

No Mix

This happened to me once when I forgot to replace the dough beater after cleaning up after making the previous loaf. Now I watch the initial mix for a minute or so when I first turn on the machine. You can see the mixing taking place. If the motor is running, but no mixing is occurring, check the dough beater. If it has been left out, stop the machine, insert the beater, and start the cycle over.

Inconsistent Size & Texture

If you bake the same recipe at different times and then get different results, blame the weather. Weather is actually a large factor in baking, as temperature and humidity influence the amount of rising that takes place. Make notes as you bake and you'll soon learn to make seasonal adjustments for your particular climate.

Lost Dough Beater

If you have the type of machine whose beater stays in the loaf when the bread is removed from the baking pan, check the last loaf of bread. I had a loaf of bread ready to give to a friend for testing, only to realize that I was about to give away the dough beater, too! Clean your pan right away and put everything back in the machine. Then your beater will always be where you want it: in the pan ready for baking.

CONVERTING EXISTING RECIPES

After you've gotten used to your bread machine, you will probably want to try out some of your favorite recipes. However, when you look them over, you will see that they weren't designed to work in a bread machine. But, fortunately, most yeast-bread recipes can be converted to work in bread machines.

The key is to make sure that the recipe is yeast-based. Although today yeast is reliable and easy to use, this was not always the case. Thus, recipes that are more than 40 or 50 years old will likely use chemical, rather than organic, leavening. Chemical leavenings include baking soda and baking powder, and they do not have the same properties as yeast. Don't attempt to convert recipes that are not yeast-based for use in your bread machine.

Converting a standard bread recipe to work in your machine isn't difficult, but it is computationally intensive work. Therefore, have a calculator handy if you want to attempt a conversion. You'll also want a sheet or two of paper to write down the totals and the new, converted recipe.

This chapter will teach you to convert a standard recipe to one you can try in your machine. It may take one or two trials to perfect the recipe, but the chances are good that you can successfully make the conversion. Before converting a recipe, make sure that it's a yeast-bread recipe. As mentioned before, most bread machines are not designed to handle breads using chemically based leavenings, nor are they designed for "quick breads." Often called "batter breads," these are breads whose batter is of a consistency similar to pancake batter.

Four Basic Steps

1. Cut the recipe down so that it will make one loaf. Many recipes are designed to make two loaves. You'll need to cut such recipes in half for a single loaf.
2. Be familiar with the working and capacities of your particular bread machine.
3. Determine the liquidity ratio of the recipe. This ratio represents the "stiffness" of the dough. This is an important factor, because your machine has a rather narrow range of dough consistencies it can handle.
4. Determine the overall bulk of the recipe. You don't want a recipe that's too large for your machine.

Let's look at each of these steps in more detail. Once you have accomplished a few conversions, you won't need to refer to this book, because the steps aren't as complex as they might seem at first.

Step 1—Reducing Recipe Size

Most recipes indicate how many loaves they make. Some will even indicate the approximate size of each loaf. Cut the recipe down so that it will make one loaf, and write down the new recipe.

If the recipe doesn't say how many loaves it makes, make a rough judgment by looking at the amount of flour required. A 1-pound loaf of bread will require about 2 cups of flour. Thus, if your recipe calls for 6 cups of all-purpose flour, you can probably figure that it will make three 1-pound loaves or two 1½-pound loaves.

Step 2—Determining the Machine's Capacity & Power

Since each machine varies in its capacity and motor power, you must determine the acceptable ranges for your machine in two categories: liquidity ratio and bulk. Table 2 shows the acceptable liquidity-ratio ranges. To find your machine's

Table 2—Bread-Machine Liquidity Ratios

Ounces Liquid ⅛ c = 1 oz	Cups of Flour			
	2	2½	3	3½
5	2.9–3.5	3.6–4.4	4.3–5.3	5.0–6.2
6	2.4–3.0	3.0–3.6	3.6–4.4	4.2–5.2
7	2.1–2.5	2.6–3.2	3.1–3.7	3.6–4.4
8	1.8–2.2	2.3–2.8	2.7–3.3	3.2–3.9
9	1.6–2.0	2.0–2.4	2.4–3.0	2.8–3.4
10	1.4–1.8	1.8–2.2	2.2–2.6	2.5–3.1
11	1.4–1.7	1.6–2.0	2.0–2.4	2.3–2.8

Notes: 1. Shaded boxes show the most common bread-machine ratio ranges. 2. Ratio is computed by dividing dry ingredients by liquid. 3. Higher ratios indicate stiffer dough; lower ratios indicate more liquid dough.

range, look at the basic white-bread recipe that came with your machine. Determine the number of cups of flour called for. Follow that column until you find the row that shows the number of ounces of liquid (water or milk) called for in the recipe. In that box you will find the ratio range for your machine.

Highlight or write down that ratio range. (On page 125, you can note this and other information about your bread machine.)

Bulk is determined by the number of cups of flour called for in the basic white-bread recipe for your machine. If the recipe calls for 2 to 2½ cups of flour,

Table 3—Dough Liquidity Calculation Worksheet

Ingredient	DRY			WET			
	tsp	tbs	cup	tsp	tbs	cup	oz
Subtotal							
Multiplier		3	48		3	48	6
TOTAL							
GRAND TOTAL							
Liquidity Ratio							

Instructions: 1. Use decimals for fractions (.5 teaspoon, etc.). 2. Use a calculator to subtotal each column. 3. Multiply the subtotal by the multiplier to obtain the total. 4. Add the dry totals and wet totals separately to obtain the grand total. 5. Divide the dry grand total by the wet grand total to get the liquidity ratio.

you have a 1-pound machine. If the recipe calls for 3 to 4 cups of flour, you have a 1½-pound (or greater) machine.

Once you know the capabilities of your machine, you can skip this step and move right from Step One to Step Three.

Step 3—Determining the Liquidity Ratio

Now you must determine the liquidity ratio (dough stiffness) of the recipe you're trying to convert. Table 3 can be copied and used each time you convert a recipe. To use the chart, simply fill in the ingredients and the amount called for in the original recipe. Write the amount in decimals (so that you can use your calculator to add them later) in the appropriate column. For example, if the recipe calls for 2½ cups of flour, enter 2.5 in the DRY cup column. You will have to determine whether the ingredient is dry or wet. In general, use the form that the ingredient is in when you add it. An exception to this would be an ingredient that is going to melt when heat is applied. Typical ingredients in this category would include butter, margarine, fresh cheeses, and shortening.

Some ingredients shouldn't be computed. In addition to yeast, don't include raisins, nuts, or seeds added at the mix cycle in the calculation. Count raisins, nuts, and seeds added initially as dry ingredients. The general rule is that if the dry ingredient will add to the stiffness of the dough, count it as a dry ingredient.

After you've entered all the ingredients, total each column and place the sum in the subtotal box. Then multiply each subtotal by the multiplier specified and place the result in the total box. Add the totals for the dry ingredients together for a grand total and do the same for wet ingredients. Finally, divide the dry grand total by the wet grand total to compute the ratio for this recipe.

For best results, the ratio should fall within the liquidity-ratio-range designation for your machine (see Step Two). If this ratio only misses by a few points, it will probably be satisfactory. If the ratio for the recipe is below the range, your dough might be too wet. Try a slight reduction in liquid ingredients or an increase in dry ingredients and recalculate. If the ratio is above the range, it is too dry. Either reduce the dry ingredients slightly or add liquid.

Chances are that you'll still need to experiment to get the recipe just right, but this calculation will give you a good start and place you well beyond the "trial-and-error" stage.

Step 4—Determining Bulk

You certainly don't want to overflow your machine with your test recipe, so make sure the bulk doesn't exceed the capacity of your machine. If you have a 1-pound machine, your recipe shouldn't call for more than 2½ cups of flour. A 1½-pound machine is limited to about 3½ cups of flour. If you need to fine-tune the recipe, make sure you make equal adjustments to both the wet and dry ingredients to maintain the liquidity ratio of the recipe.

Improving & Tailoring Your Recipes

After you first attempt a newly converted recipe, you may want to adjust the recipe to increase or decrease the bulk, reduce or increase rise, or alter the texture or taste. Experiment with the recipe until you've perfected it. Part of the enjoyment of using a bread machine is being able to try new and exciting recipes and to be creative. Although the conversion process, as presented here, may seem better suited to a mathematician than to an artist, science and art go hand-in-hand in bread baking. Once you get to know your machine and your ingredients, you'll feel comfortable making substitutions or even trying brand-new creations from stratch.

RECIPE POINTERS

Recipe Sizes

Two sizes are given for each of the recipes in this book. Smaller sizes are possible, but I don't recommend them. In experimenting, I found that the machines tended to overbake ¾-pound loaves and that these loaves typically were too dry. Consequently, I decided to include only the two sizes that can be accommodated by virtually all bread machines.

Recipe sizes refer to finished weight, not dimensions. The finished dimensions of the bread will depend to a great extent on baking conditions, amount of yeast used, and types of ingredients. A 1-pound loaf of white bread, for example, might be larger than a 1½-pound loaf of rye bread, because rye tends to be more densely textured than white.

Modifications for Specific Machines

I tried to include recipes that would work in any machine. With the 1-pound recipes, I found virtually no difference when testing the recipes in different machines. With the 1½-pound loaves, however, I noted that some machines will not tolerate a stiff dough as well as others. For those recipes, I have noted that you might consider adding 1 or 2 tablespoons more liquid in certain machines. This addition will lower the liquidity ratio slightly, making the dough less stiff. Some machine motors appear to labor under the load of 1½ pounds of stiff dough. If your machine seems to be having trouble kneading dough, add a little liquid to the recipe. As mentioned previously, you will come to recognize the normal sounds of your machine and be able to identify those situations when slight recipe modifications are needed.

The other major difference among machines has to do with their rise cycles and the amount of yeast called for. I tried to optimize the amount of yeast in the recipes to be suitable to all machines. When more yeast is needed for a certain type of machine, such as one with a yeast dispenser, the notes for the recipe will indicate this addition.

Many machines have a quick-bread cycle that allows you to bake a loaf faster (single rise, rather than the usual double rise). When using this cycle on your machine, double the amount of yeast that is normally called for or consult your owner's manual for the proper yeast adjustment.

23

Ingredients

A wide variety of ingredients is called for in these recipes. Many are available at your local supermarket, but some must be bought at health-food stores. What follows is a summary of important information about some of the main ingredients used in the recipes in this book.

White Flours

There are two main types of white flours: all-purpose flour and bread flour. Both varieties are available in most grocery stores. Bread flour is slightly higher in gluten content than all-purpose flour, and it will usually rise more. Most of the recipes in this book call for bread flour; however, a few specifically call for all-purpose flour. Substituting all-purpose flour for bread flour is permissible, but it may slightly change the texture of the bread and cause it to rise less.

Whole Grains

Whole-wheat flour This flour is ground from the complete wheat berry and contains the wheat germ and the wheat bran. It is coarser and heavier than white flour, and it doesn't rise as much. I buy fresh wheat in bulk and grind it myself for the best-tasting bread, although this is beyond the capability of most people. Grocery stores carry whole-wheat flour, usually alongside white flour.

Graham flour In the early 1900s, Sylvester Graham publicly argued the merits of grains in the diet, and wheat in particular. Graham flour is essentially equivalent to whole-wheat flour, except that it is slightly coarser and has larger particles of bran throughout. This gives it a flavor that's sweeter than whole-wheat flour. In recipes calling for graham flour, freely substitute whole-wheat flour if graham flour isn't available.

Semolina flour This is whole-grain durum wheat with the bran layer removed. It can be used for bread making, particularly in combination with bread flour.

Bran Bran is the outer covering of the kernel of wheat or oat. It is rich in fibre and is called for in small quantities in some recipes. Recently, much has been said about the benefits of oat bran. Both oat and wheat bran are available at most grocery stores.

Wheat germ This part of the wheat grain is readily available in grocery stores. As with bran, it is used sparingly in recipes. Wheat germ should be kept in the refrigerator after the container is opened.

Rye flour Rye flour is very low in gluten content, and it will not rise when used by itself. You will notice that most of the rye-bread recipes in this book also call for another flour with a higher gluten content, which will allow the bread to rise.

Barley flour Barley flour gives a sweet taste and smooth texture to bread. Most recipes call for it in combination with white or wheat flour, because it has no gluten content. You'll probably have to go to a health-food store to find barley flour.

Cracked wheat As its name implies, this is part of the wheat berry. It is very hard and usually requires some soaking before use. Cracked wheat is widely available at health-food stores and can often also be found in grocery stores.

Seven-grain cereal This cereal has an appearance similar to cracked wheat. It consists of seven grains, including wheat, barley, corn, and oats. It is available at health-food stores.

Oats Use rolled oats (oatmeal) for your oat recipes. Just use the type available at the grocery store. When measuring rolled oats, pack them down into the measuring cup to get a full measure.

Quinoa This flour is imported from South America and was a staple grain of the Incas in ancient times. Quinoa has one of the highest protein contents of any grain. It gives bread a somewhat nutty flavor.

Buckwheat flour Despite its name, this flour is not made from wheat. Buckwheat is actually a grass that yields a groat called kasha, which can then be ground into flour. It is usually used in small quantities, but if you like its strong flavor, you can use it in combination with whole-wheat flour.

Soy flour This flour is ground from toasted soybeans and is high in protein content at about 40 to 50 percent. It is very nutritious, but not flavorful, and is often used for enriching the nutritional value of bread.

Millet This small, yellow grain can be used in bread whole, either raw or cooked, or milled into flour.

Rice Rice can be cooked and added to bread or made into flour. The flour absorbs moisture more slowly than most other flours, so it is well known among bakers as an excellent flour for dusting breads.

Liquids

Water Water is called for in most recipes. It should be used warm, between 100 and 110°F (38 and 43°C). Hot tap water works fine. Don't heat the water any further, because water that's too hot can kill the yeast.

Milk When milk is called for in a recipe, I use 1-percent-fat, or skim, milk. In fact, the nutritional counts in the recipes in this book are calculated using values for 1-percent-fat milk. If you don't have fresh milk on hand, try using dry milk and adding the requisite amount of water to the recipe. Milk should usually be warmed to 100 to 110°F (38 to 43°C). The microwave heats milk well at 45 seconds on HIGH. Be careful not to add overheated milk to the mix, or you'll kill the yeast.

Buttermilk You can use buttermilk in its fresh form or buy buttermilk powder and mix it as needed. I do the latter, because I don't particularly like to drink buttermilk and recipes usually only call for small amounts. In most recipes, it is safe to substitute low-fat or skim milk for buttermilk. You may sacrifice some flavor, but your bread will have a lower fat content.

Cream There are several types of cream available at most grocery stores:

heavy cream, light cream, whipping cream, and half-and-half. Some recipes call for heavy or light cream, but I have found that whipping cream works fine in most cases. Note that *whipping cream* and *whipped cream* are different. Whipped cream has added sugar and is already whipped. Whipping cream comes in a carton and pours like milk.

Eggs Most of the recipes in this book have been formulated to call for whole eggs, rather than portions of eggs or egg whites only. However, if you're concerned about the cholesterol in eggs, you may use any commercially available egg substitute. Use ¼ cup (4 tablespoons) of egg substitute in place of each whole egg. If you use powdered eggs, use ¼ cup of mixed powdered eggs instead of one whole egg.

Butter Although many of the recipes in this book call for butter, you may substitute margarine or vegetable oil in the same quantity. Butter, however, will provide the most flavor. I keep butter in the freezer, because spoilage is a real problem with butter. When I need butter, I remove it from the freezer, cut off the required quantity, and replace the stick in the freezer. It only takes a few minutes for the cut portion to reach room temperature. There's no need to melt the butter or margarine before adding either to a recipe, but it is best if the chunks are 1 tablespoon or less in size.

Olive oil I use olive oil exclusively in these recipes, instead of other oils. I think olive oil tastes best and it has no cholesterol. However, if you prefer another type of cooking oil, such as canola, corn oil, or any other vegetable oil, you may substitute it freely. If you use olive oil, use a good grade of extra-virgin olive oil.

Other Ingredients

Salt Salt is a yeast inhibitor, and it's necessary in most recipes. If you are on a salt-restricted diet, eliminate the salt from the recipes. If you do so, the characteristics of the bread will change. The bread will rise differently, and it may rise too much and then collapse. The resulting texture may also be different. Keep in mind that other ingredients often have a salt content. If you are on a salt-restricted diet, check the nutritional values for each recipe to see if it contains "hidden salts." Butter, for example is one of the ingredients that has a sodium content. Avoid using salt substitutes as alternatives. They are chemically based and do not have the yeast-inhibiting properties of real salt. They may also cause other chemical reactions that will change the properties of your bread.

Yeast The recipes in this book call for yeast in teaspoons. I use active dry yeast, and I buy it in bulk. If kept in the refrigerator, it will last a long time, but with my bread machine running, a supply of yeast doesn't last long at all. If you use cake yeast, make the conversion from teaspoons. If you buy yeast in packets at the grocery store, one packet contains one scant tablespoon or about 2¼ teaspoons. Don't use rapid-rise yeast in these recipes.

Not all bread machines use the same amount of yeast in the large recipes. This is due to differences in cycle lengths and the yeast-dispensing mechanisms on a few machines. If a recipe doesn't rise enough, try adding an extra ½ teaspoon of yeast.

Yeast feeds on sugars and is inhibited by salts. It likes a warm environment, but too much heat will kill it. Most traditional bread recipes will require you to "proof" your yeast before using it. Proofing involves mixing the yeast with sugar and warm (105 to 110°F [41 to 43°C]) water to allow it to become active before adding it to the recipe. Proofing is not necessary with bread machines, but it is a good technique to use if you want to make sure your yeast is still active (not too old). Yeast can be placed directly into the bread pan. When it touches liquid, it will begin activating.

Sugars & sweeteners These are necessary in all bread recipes because they provide food for the yeast. Recipes in this book call for sugar (white, granulated, or brown), honey, syrup, or molasses. Molasses comes in various types, but I use blackstrap when baking. I've tried others, and I haven't noticed any appreciable difference in the outcome, so use any molasses you happen to have on hand. If a recipe calls for olive oil and honey or molasses, measure the olive oil first and don't rinse off the spoon. The honey or molasses will slide right off the spoon into your pan!

Gluten Gluten is necessary for rising to occur. White flours contain plenty of gluten, but some whole-grain breads do not. I have found that adding some gluten flour to the mix when using a low-gluten flour will make for better rising and texture. Gluten flour can be bought at most health-food stores. Although a few recipes call for gluten flour, it is optional in most. Some people are allergic to gluten. Therefore, they should stick to low-gluten flours, such as rye and quinoa.

Dough enhancer This product is difficult to find. Even health-food stores may not carry it. You may find it at baking specialty stores. Dough enhancer is a powder produced from *tofu* (soybean) that makes the dough smoother. Commercial bakers often use dough enhancer to obtain the smooth-textured bread you buy at the store. If you want to try it, it's listed as an optional ingredient in some of the recipes.

Spices, nuts, & seeds These ingredients are called for in a wide variety of recipes. I have found most of them at the grocery store. But, if you can't find them there, you might try a large health-food store, which will usually stock some of the lesser known spices. Feel free to experiment with spices, adding more of the spices that you like and omitting those that you don't. Often it is the blend of spices that makes the flavor, rather than any single spice, especially in those recipes calling for two or three different kinds.

You'll find that as you bake more breads, the spices in your cabinet will proliferate. Eventually, you will have a stock of almost any spice called for in a recipe. Preserving spices and seeds is not a problem, but preserving fresh nuts is. A few recipes call for fresh chopped nuts. Use any types of nut you like, but keep in mind that nuts will go rancid if not used in a short period, so keep your supply of fresh nuts rotated.

Sourdough starter There is a recipe for sourdough starter on pages 31–33. You can use this recipe, locate another (any good bread-recipe book will have one), or simply get starter from your local bakery or from a friend. Once you have starter going, you can keep it replenished and never run short. Starter is used in sourdough recipes and can be added as you would any other ingredients.

Order of Ingredients

There are two ways to place ingredients in the baking pan: either dry ingredients first or wet ingredients first. Most machines call for dry ingredients first, so that order is used in this book. Actually, dry first will work in all machines, unless you want to use a timed-bake function. In that case, you won't want to activate the yeast until the baking process starts, so the wet ingredients will have to go first and the yeast last. The machines that recommend dry ingredients first call for yeast as the first ingredient, followed by the other dry ingredients and, finally, the liquids. That is the order followed in these recipes. If your machine calls for wet ingredients first or if you want to use a timed-bake feature, add the ingredients to the pan in reverse order from that listed (start at the bottom of the list and work your way to the top).

Preparation of Ingredients

Most bread recipes call for all ingredients to be at room temperature, except for liquids, which are sometimes called for at 105 to 110°F (41 to 43°C). I experimented with this and have not had any real problems adding refrigerated ingredients. Rather than worry too much about it, just try setting all of your ingredients out first and then add them. Once you get to the refrigerated ingredients, they've usually approached room temperature.

When warm water is called for, it should be in the 105 to 110°F (41 to 43°C) range. I used to use a thermometer to make sure that the water was the correct temperature, but I soon gave up on that when I found that hot tap water usually falls within that range. Hot tap water varies, however; so make sure that yours is not too hot. (Too hot presents a much bigger problem than too cold.)

Milk can either be measured and then left to reach room temperature, or you can use the microwave to warm it up. Just be sure that if you use the microwave, you don't overheat the milk, which is easy to do. If you do overheat it, let it sit until it cools to 110°F (43°C) or cooler before adding it to the bread pan.

For measuring flour and other dry ingredients, I use the dip-and-level method, rather than a spoon. Simply dip your measuring cup into the flour, and level it with a knife or other flat edge.

Substitutions & Modifications

I recommend that you try the recipes as is the first time. Then if you want to make substitutions or modifications, experiment all you want. I have found that the best way to experiment is to alter one item at a time. If you alter too many things at once and the recipe fails, you won't be able to determine the cause of the failure. However, if you only changed one ingredient, you will know that that was the only variable that could have caused the failure.

You can freely make the substitutions mentioned in the "Ingredients" section, including margarine for butter, low-fat or skim milk for buttermilk, egg substitutes for whole eggs, and all-purpose flour for bread flour. Keep in mind, however, that these substitutions will alter the original recipe somewhat and results will be different.

Avoid the use of chemically based substitutes, such as sugar and salt substitutes. These chemically based products may taste the same in coffee or soft drinks, but they break down differently from real sodium or sugar in baking and they won't work properly with yeast breads. It is better simply to eliminate salt, for example, than to use a salt substitute. Yeast feeds well on sugar, but it doesn't thrive on aspartame.

Once you have a feel for a recipe and for your machine, feel free to experiment. The recipes in this book were developed that way, and you can enjoy yourself trying new and wonderful ideas. Begin with established recipes and make successive alterations until you arrive at the perfect bread. Be sure to keep a log of your changes and the results. That way, you can learn as you go and you won't repeat mistakes. It also helps to have a basic understanding of the principles of baking with yeast and the characteristics of the ingredients you're using.

Slicing Bread

When you get a loaf out of the machine, it smells wonderful. In fact, it has probably permeated the whole house with the unmistakable aroma of baking bread! You may want to dig in and eat the whole loaf right on the spot. Of course, you can do that. There is nothing better than fresh hot bread. However, if your aim is to slice the bread and keep it for a few days, then you'll need to slice it carefully.

Bread is best sliced after it's had a chance to cool completely. It then regains some of its stiffness and is much easier to handle. Slicing hot bread is a bit like trying to slice Jell-O. As you cut, the bread gives, and it is difficult to get a good straight slice.

For best results, remove your bread from the machine as soon as the all-done alarm sounds. Place the bread on a cooling rack and let it cool completely (probably an hour or so). While many machines now include cooling cycles, they can't completely cool the bread because the loaf is still in the pan, where moisture and heat are trapped.

To slice bread, use a serrated knife designed especially for such a task. Use a sawing motion and let the knife do the work. Putting too much downward pressure on the bread will smash it down and give you uneven slices.

I have a meat slicer, but I don't use it for meat at all. I *have* found it to be a wonderful bread slicer. All you need to do is set the thickness and the serrated blade cuts right through the cool loaf. If you have a slicer and your loaf is too large for it (the Welbilt loaves are too large for mine), cut the loaf in half lengthwise, making two half-circles. Then slice each half-loaf with your slicer.

Nutritional Values

Much of the consumer motivation behind the boom in bread-machine sales is due to a desire to eat more healthful foods. Whole-grain breads are wonderful sources of nutrients, have no chemical preservatives, and they taste great.

Each recipe in this book is followed by a nutritional analysis. I have purposely set the nutritional values at the level of one loaf, rather than determine the values of a single slice. Everyone will slice bread differently. If you want to know the nutritional value for a slice of bread, estimate what percentage of the total loaf the slice is and multiply that number by the nutritional values shown for the size you baked. For example, a 1½-pound loaf is cut into 10 slices, multiply the nutritional values by 0.1 to obtain the values for one slice.

The nutritional values are estimates only, and they shouldn't be construed as anything else. They were derived from the *Encyclopedia of Food Values*, by Corinne T. Netzer (Dell, 1992). Each of the ingredients in the recipes was calculated and totalled for each size of loaf. What follows is an explanation of the values asked:

Calories are total calories for the loaf.

Protein is measured in grams. Breads are not high in protein content, but when taken with other foods (for example, meats, or legumes such as beans) that are high in protein, a healthful combination is made.

Carbohydrates are also measured in grams. Carbohydrates, especially from whole-grain sources, provide a good ratio of nutrients to calories (the opposite of "empty calories") and should constitute 45 to 48 percent of our daily intake of calories.

Fat is listed as total fat and saturated fat. We should try to reduce the amount of fats in our diet, and saturated fats should be avoided as much as possible. According to government recommendations, we should limit our total calories from fat to 30 percent of our daily intake of calories, and saturated-fat calories to only 10 percent. In addition to giving you the amount of total fat and saturated fat in grams, I have computed the percentage of calories from fat for each recipe. You will notice that these breads are very healthful from the standpoint of percentage of calories from fats.

Cholesterol is measured in milligrams. Cholesterol is found only in animal fats and certain vegetable fats (such as palm oil and coconut oil). Most nutritionists recommend that your total dietary cholesterol intake not exceed 300 milligrams per day.

Sodium, measured in milligrams, can be found not only in the salt added to the recipe, but also in some of the other recipe ingredients. If you are on a low-sodium diet, you can reduce the salt content of the loaf, but remember the ramifications discussed earlier.

Fibre is a growing concern to health-conscious people. The fibre content of each recipe is measured in grams. Because fibre takes several forms, the figure given is a total figure that includes both dietary and crude fibre. Most nutritionists recommend at least 25 grams of fibre per day in your diet.

Recipe Notes

Some recipes contain notes regarding variations to be used with certain machines. These notes refer to *classes* of machines. If the note mentions low-power machines, it refers to any machine calling for 1¼ cups of liquid, 3 cups of flour, and 1 package of yeast in its basic 1½-pound white-bread recipe. Your machine might also fall into this category if you notice that the motor labors with stiff doughs. References to yeast-dispensing machines include any machine calling for 1¼ cups of liquid, 3 cups of flour, and 3 teaspoons of yeast in its basic 1½-pound white-bread recipe. These variations usually only apply to the 1½-pound recipes, although occasionally I have made an alteration for a 1-pound recipe.

Your strategy for testing recipes should be to try the 1-pound loaf first, even if you have a 1½-pound-capacity machine. This offers you three advantages:

1. You can ensure that you like the taste and texture of the bread by using a lesser quantity of ingredients for the first test.
2. You can ensure that the bread works well in your machine with fewer ingredients at risk.
3. You can ensure that your particular baking conditions will not produce an oversize loaf, with little risk of a mess if they do.

Once you've tested a bread, alter the recipe to suit your taste, baking conditions, and machine. For example, you can increase or reduce yeast amounts, alter the liquidity, try substitute seeds or nuts, or substitute other ingredients. Try the recipe once as published here before you modify them. This will give you a basis upon which to make your changes and a point of reference. Then, be creative.

Sourdough Breads

Some of the recipes in this volume call for sourdough starter or sourdough batter. Here are recipes for both.

Sourdough Starter

Sourdough starter is a type of sponge that is created and then used and fed continuously, sometimes over a period of many years. This recipe will give you enough starter for you to begin. Each time you remove the starter to make batter, don't forget to replenish the starter with your leftover batter. Starter is best stored in the refrigerator in a glass container. It improves with age. The older the starter, the more pungent the taste and aroma. Starter age is measured in years, not days, so don't become impatient with your starter. As it matures, it will get better and better.

- Warm a quart jar or similar container by filling it with hot tap water and letting it sit for a few minutes.
- In a pan or microwave oven, heat one cup of skim or low-fat milk to 100 to 110°F (38 to 43°C). Then remove the milk from the heat and add 3 tablespoons of plain yogurt to the milk.
- Drain the warm water that has been heating your starter jar, and wipe the jar dry.
- Pour the milk-yogurt mixture into the jar and cover it. Use a plastic lid, but if your jar has a metal lid, place plastic wrap or waxed paper under the lid before screwing the lid tight.
- Place the mixture in a warm place and allow it to proof for 24 hours.
- After the mixture has proofed, stir 1 cup of all-purpose flour into the milk-yogurt mixture. Cover and leave in a warm place for 3 to 5 days.
- After about 5 days, your starter should be bubbly and about the consistency of pancake batter. When it has reached this point, place the jar in the refrigerator for storage.

Sourdough Starter Batter

Even with a bread machine, sourdough-bread recipes require a little more patience than other bread recipes because the sourdough batter must be prepared in advance. Here is the procedure for making sourdough batter for any recipe requiring sourdough starter.

- Remove the sourdough starter from the refrigerator, and allow it to reach room temperature (about 6 hours).
- Place 1½ cups of starter in a 2-quart mixing bowl.
- Return the remaining starter to the refrigerator.
- Add 1½ cups of all-purpose flour and 1 cup of warm skim milk and mix well. The batter should have the consistency of light pancake batter.
- Cover the bowl lightly and let the batter proof for 8 to 12 hours in an 85 to 90°F (30 to 32°C) environment.
- After proofing, use what batter you need for your bread (the batter can remain out for 1 to 3 days), but make sure to save at least 1½ cups of batter to replenish your starter.
- Return the remaining batter to your starter pot. Stir and refrigerate.

Many people will place the starter directly into the bread ingredients. While this method will certainly work, it is not the best way to keep your starter active, because after you remove the starter, you have to add flour and milk and again proof the starter.

I have found it better to use the batter method just described. It tends to keep the starter more active and yields plenty of batter to use in my recipes. If you use the batter method, place the batter in the recipe any time sourdough starter is called for.

Disclaimer

The nutritional values shown with the recipes in this book are approximations only and are shown strictly for comparison. Because nutritional values will vary according to the product brand, quantity, and type of ingredient used, individuals needing specific nutrient values should compute the values themselves. Neither the author nor the publisher represents these values to reflect the exact nutritional content of these recipes.

Results of these recipes will vary according to climatic conditions, proper use of ingredients, make and model of machine used, and freshness of ingredients. All recipes in this book have been thoroughly tested but not on all available machines. The author and publisher make no guarantee as to the results of an individual recipe baked on a particular machine in a specific situation, since the possible combinations of variables are almost endless.

WHITE BREADS

The recipes in this section are all variations of white bread. They are typically finely textured and high rising, and they go well with just about any other food. The breads range from slightly sweet to spicy to fruity. Experiment with the recipes by substituting the fruits, nuts, and spices of your choice.

Argentine Easter Bread

This festive bread makes a great breakfast toast and is particularly good with jam or jelly.

1½-pound

1 teaspoon active dry yeast

2¾ cups bread flour

1 teaspoon salt

½ teaspoon dried lemon peel

½ teaspoon dried orange peel

3½ tablespoons sugar

3 eggs

2½ tablespoons butter

4 ounces warm milk

¾ cup raisins

1-pound

½ teaspoon active dry yeast

1¾ cups bread flour

½ teaspoon salt

¼ teaspoon dried lemon peel

¼ teaspoon dried orange peel

2½ tablespoons sugar

2 eggs

1½ tablespoons butter

3 ounces warm milk

½ cup raisins

Notes:

1. For machines with yeast dispensers, use 2 teaspoons of yeast for the 1½-pound loaf.
2. Raisins can be added at the mix-cycle beep, if your machine is so equipped.

NUTRITIONAL ANALYSIS			
	1½-POUND	1-POUND	
TOTAL CALORIES	2330	1502	
TOTAL PROTEIN	69	44	GRAMS
TOTAL CARBOHYDRATES	404	263	GRAMS
TOTAL FAT	50	31	GRAMS
TOTAL SATURATED FAT	24	14	GRAMS
TOTAL CHOLESTEROL	717	473	MILLIGRAMS
TOTAL SODIUM	2344	1207	MILLIGRAMS
TOTAL FIBRE	12	8	GRAMS
% CALORIES FROM FAT	19	19	

Babovka

This sweet, lightly textured Czech bread is best served hot, sprinkled with a mixture of powdered sugar and cinnamon.

1½-pound

1 teaspoon active dry yeast

3 cups bread flour

½ teaspoon salt

5 tablespoons brown sugar

7 ounces warm milk

2 egg yolks

5 tablespoons butter

½ cup raisins

1-pound

½ teaspoon active dry yeast

2 cups bread flour

¼ teaspoon salt

3 tablespoons brown sugar

5 ounces warm milk

1 egg yolk

3 tablespoons butter

⅓ cup raisins

Notes:

1. For machines with yeast dispensers, use 2 teaspoons of yeast for the 1½-pound loaf.
2. Raisins can be added at the mix-cycle beep, if your machine is so equipped.

NUTRITIONAL ANALYSIS			
	1½-POUND	1-POUND	
TOTAL CALORIES	2203	1428	
TOTAL PROTEIN	72	46	GRAMS
TOTAL CARBOHYDRATES	434	285	GRAMS
TOTAL FAT	20	11	GRAMS
TOTAL SATURATED FAT	6	3	GRAMS
TOTAL CHOLESTEROL	435	219	MILLIGRAMS
TOTAL SODIUM	1336	695	MILLIGRAMS
TOTAL FIBRE	10	7	GRAMS
% CALORIES FROM FAT	8	7	

Belgian Molasses Bread

The molasses and the light wheat flavors give this bread a unique aroma and taste. Try it instead of rye bread.

1½-pound

1½ teaspoons active dry yeast

2½ cups bread flour

1 teaspoon salt

½ cup whole-wheat flour

1 tablespoon butter

4 tablespoons molasses

¾ cup warm milk

2½ ounces warm water

1-pound

1 teaspoon active dry yeast

1½ cups bread flour

1 teaspoon salt

½ cup whole-wheat flour

1 tablespoon butter

2 tablespoons molasses

½ cup warm milk

3 tablespoons warm water

Note:

For machines with yeast dispensers, use 3 teaspoons of yeast for the 1½-pound loaf.

NUTRITIONAL ANALYSIS			
	1½-POUND	1-POUND	
TOTAL CALORIES	1868	1254	
TOTAL PROTEIN	57	38	GRAMS
TOTAL CARBOHYDRATES	358	234	GRAMS
TOTAL FAT	20	17	GRAMS
TOTAL SATURATED FAT	9	9	GRAMS
TOTAL CHOLESTEROL	39	36	MILLIGRAMS
TOTAL SODIUM	2293	2237	MILLIGRAMS
TOTAL FIBRE	13	11	GRAMS
% CALORIES FROM FAT	10	12	

Buttermilk & Honey Bread

This traditional farm bread is a good white-bread staple, making it excellent for sandwiches or toast.

1½-pound

1 teaspoon active dry yeast

3 cups bread flour

1½ teaspoons salt

½ teaspoon sugar

1½ tablespoons honey

1 tablespoon butter

¾ cup buttermilk

3 ounces warm water

1-pound

½ teaspoon active dry yeast

2 cups bread flour

1 teaspoon salt

½ teaspoon sugar

1 tablespoon honey

1 tablespoon butter

3 ounces buttermilk

3 ounces warm water

Note:

For machines with yeast dispensers, use 2 teaspoons of yeast for the 1½-pound loaf.

NUTRITIONAL ANALYSIS			
	1½-POUND	1-POUND	
TOTAL CALORIES	1777	1205	
TOTAL PROTEIN	58	37	GRAMS
TOTAL CARBOHYDRATES	336	223	GRAMS
TOTAL FAT	20	17	GRAMS
TOTAL SATURATED FAT	9	8	GRAMS
TOTAL CHOLESTEROL	47	39	MILLIGRAMS
TOTAL SODIUM	3323	2196	MILLIGRAMS
TOTAL FIBRE	6	4	GRAMS
% CALORIES FROM FAT	10	12	

Buttermilk Potato Bread

The potato and buttermilk make this a richer-than-normal white bread. It's excellent with soup.

1½-pound

1½ teaspoons active dry yeast

3 cups bread flour

1½ teaspoons salt

1 tablespoon sugar

3 tablespoons instant mashed-
  potato flakes or buds

5 ounces warm water

1 tablespoon butter

½ cup buttermilk

1-pound

1 teaspoon active dry yeast

2 cups bread flour

1 teaspoon salt

2 teaspoons sugar

2 tablespoons instant mashed-
  potato flakes or buds

3½ ounces warm water

½ tablespoon butter

⅓ cup buttermilk

Note:

For machines with yeast dispensers, use 3 teaspoons of yeast for the 1½-pound loaf.

NUTRITIONAL ANALYSIS			
	1½-POUND	1-POUND	
TOTAL CALORIES	1748	1183	
TOTAL PROTEIN	57	41	GRAMS
TOTAL CARBOHYDRATES	325	221	GRAMS
TOTAL FAT	22	13	GRAMS
TOTAL SATURATED FAT	9	5	GRAMS
TOTAL CHOLESTEROL	41	28	MILLIGRAMS
TOTAL SODIUM	3420	2325	MILLIGRAMS
TOTAL FIBRE	7	4	GRAMS
% CALORIES FROM FAT	11	10	

Danish Buttermilk Bread

The ground caraway seeds in this recipe give this buttermilk bread its singular flavor.

1½-pound

1½ teaspoons active dry yeast

2 teaspoons ground caraway seeds

3 cups bread flour

1½ teaspoons salt

1 tablespoon brown sugar

5 ounces buttermilk

3 tablespoons butter

3 ounces warm water

1-pound

1 teaspoon active dry yeast

1 teaspoon ground caraway seeds

2 cups bread flour

1 teaspoon salt

1 tablespoon brown sugar

3 ounces buttermilk

2½ tablespoons butter

¼ cup warm water

Notes:

1. For machines with yeast dispensers, use 3 teaspoons of yeast for the 1½-pound loaf.
2. For machines with low-power motors, add 2 extra tablespoons of warm water to the 1½-pound recipe.

NUTRITIONAL ANALYSIS			
	1½-POUND	1-POUND	
TOTAL CALORIES	1933	1349	
TOTAL PROTEIN	58	38	GRAMS
TOTAL CARBOHYDRATES	324	220	GRAMS
TOTAL FAT	43	34	GRAMS
TOTAL SATURATED FAT	23	19	GRAMS
TOTAL CHOLESTEROL	106	85	MILLIGRAMS
TOTAL SODIUM	3310	2202	MILLIGRAMS
TOTAL FIBRE	7	5	GRAMS
% CALORIES FROM FAT	20	23	

Dutch Prune Bread

A fruity flavor makes this bread great toasted or with fruit jams or jellies.

1½-pound

1½ teaspoons active dry yeast

3¼ cups bread flour

½ teaspoon salt

½ teaspoon cinnamon

½ teaspoon dried lemon peel

½ teaspoon dried orange peel

4 tablespoons sugar

3 tablespoons butter

1 egg

1 cup warm milk

5 tablespoons chopped prunes

1-pound

1 teaspoon active dry yeast

2¼ cups bread flour

½ teaspoon salt

½ teaspoon cinnamon

¼ teaspoon dried lemon peel

¼ teaspoon dried orange peel

2½ tablespoons sugar

2 tablespoons butter

1 egg

5 ounces warm milk

3½ tablespoons chopped prunes

Notes:

1. For machines with yeast dispensers, use 3 tablespoons of yeast for the 1½-pound loaf.
2. The prunes can be added at the mix-cycle beep, if your machine is so equipped.

NUTRITIONAL ANALYSIS			
	1½-POUND	1-POUND	
TOTAL CALORIES	2481	1672	
TOTAL PROTEIN	73	50	GRAMS
TOTAL CARBOHYDRATES	434	288	GRAMS
TOTAL FAT	50	35	GRAMS
TOTAL SATURATED FAT	26	18	GRAMS
TOTAL CHOLESTEROL	316	281	MILLIGRAMS
TOTAL SODIUM	1270	1218	MILLIGRAMS
TOTAL FIBRE	10	7	GRAMS
% CALORIES FROM FAT	18	19	

French Almond Bread

This bread has a nutty flavor combined with a slight wheat flavor, provided by the whole-wheat flour. It's richer in flavor than most other white breads.

1½-pound

1½ teaspoons active dry yeast

2 cups bread flour

1 cup chopped almonds

1 teaspoon salt

1½ tablespoons brown sugar

½ cup whole-wheat flour

¼ teaspoon walnut or almond extract

½ cup warm milk

½ cup warm water

1-pound

1 teaspoon active dry yeast

1⅓ cups bread flour

⅔ cup chopped almonds

½ teaspoon salt

1 tablespoon brown sugar

⅓ cup whole-wheat flour

¼ teaspoon walnut or almond extract

3 ounces warm milk

¼ cup warm water

Notes:

1. For machines with yeast dispensers, use 3 teaspoons of yeast for the 1½-pound loaf.
2. The chopped almonds may be added at the mix-cycle beep, if your machine is so equipped.

NUTRITIONAL ANALYSIS			
	1½-POUND	1-POUND	
TOTAL CALORIES	2102	1405	
TOTAL PROTEIN	64	43	GRAMS
TOTAL CARBOHYDRATES	292	194	GRAMS
TOTAL FAT	81	55	GRAMS
TOTAL SATURATED FAT	8	6	GRAMS
TOTAL CHOLESTEROL	5	4	MILLIGRAMS
TOTAL SODIUM	2218	1128	MILLIGRAMS
TOTAL FIBRE	18	12	GRAMS
% CALORIES FROM FAT	35	35	

Greek Easter Bread

This extra-rich white bread has a wonderful texture.

1½-pound

1 teaspoon active dry yeast

3 cups bread flour

1 teaspoon dried lemon peel

4 tablespoons sugar

½ teaspoon salt

2 eggs

8 tablespoons butter

½ cup warm milk

1-pound

½ teaspoon active dry yeast

2 cups bread flour

½ teaspoon dried lemon peel

2½ tablespoons sugar

½ teaspoon salt

1 egg

5 tablespoons butter

3 ounces warm milk

Note:

For machines with yeast dispensers, use 2 teaspoons of yeast for the 1½-pound loaf.

NUTRITIONAL ANALYSIS			
	1½-POUND	1-POUND	
TOTAL CALORIES	2677	1722	
TOTAL PROTEIN	68	43	GRAMS
TOTAL CARBOHYDRATES	354	234	GRAMS
TOTAL FAT	110	68	GRAMS
TOTAL SATURATED FAT	62	38	GRAMS
TOTAL CHOLESTEROL	679	372	MILLIGRAMS
TOTAL SODIUM	1269	1185	MILLIGRAMS
TOTAL FIBRE	6	4	GRAMS
% CALORIES FROM FAT	37	35	

Herb Cheddar Bread

The spices and cheese in this bread give it a wonderful tangy taste and moist texture. It is especially good with soup or salad.

1½-pound

1½ teaspoons active dry yeast

3 cups bread flour

1 teaspoon tarragon

1½ teaspoons chervil

1½ teaspoons basil

1 teaspoon salt

1½ teaspoons sugar

½ cup grated cheddar cheese

1½ tablespoons olive oil

7 ounces warm water

1-pound

1 teaspoon active dry yeast

2 cups + 2 tablespoons bread flour

½ teaspoon tarragon

1 teaspoon chervil

1 teaspoon basil

½ teaspoon salt

1 teaspoon sugar

⅓ cup grated cheddar cheese

1 tablespoon olive oil

5 ounces warm water

Notes:

1. For machines with yeast dispensers, use 3 teaspoons of yeast for the 1½-pound loaf.
2. The dough ball will be somewhat dry at first, but this will change as the cheese is heated and melts. For low-power motors, the motor may labor with the large recipe. If this happens, add 2 extra tablespoons of warm water.

NUTRITIONAL ANALYSIS			
	1½-POUND	1-POUND	
TOTAL CALORIES	1925	1366	
TOTAL PROTEIN	65	46	GRAMS
TOTAL CARBOHYDRATES	306	221	GRAMS
TOTAL FAT	46	31	GRAMS
TOTAL SATURATED FAT	16	10	GRAMS
TOTAL CHOLESTEROL	60	39	MILLIGRAMS
TOTAL SODIUM	2490	1303	MILLIGRAMS
TOTAL FIBRE	7	5	GRAMS
% CALORIES FROM FAT	22	20	

Honey Seed Bread

This bread feature four popular seeds. Substitute other seeds, if you like.

1½-pound

1½ teaspoons active dry yeast

3 cups bread flour

½ tablespoon sesame seeds

½ tablespoon poppy seeds

½ tablespoon fennel seeds

1 tablespoon sunflower seeds

1½ teaspoons salt

½ teaspoon sugar

1 tablespoon honey

1 tablespoon butter

9 ounces warm milk

1-pound

1 teaspoon active dry yeast

2 cups bread flour

1 teaspoon sesame seeds

1 teaspoon poppy seeds

1 teaspoon fennel seeds

2 teaspoons sunflower seeds

1 teaspoon salt

½ teaspoon sugar

½ tablespoon honey

½ tablespoon butter

¾ cup warm milk

Notes:

1. For machines with yeast dispensers, use 3 teaspoons of yeast for the 1½-pound loaf.
2. For machines with low-power motors, add 2 tablespoons of warm milk to the 1½-pound recipe.
3. Seeds may be added at the mix cycle beep, if your machine is so equipped.

NUTRITIONAL ANALYSIS			
	1½-POUND	1-POUND	
TOTAL CALORIES	1932	1295	
TOTAL PROTEIN	65	44	GRAMS
TOTAL CARBOHYDRATES	338	225	GRAMS
TOTAL FAT	34	24	GRAMS
TOTAL SATURATED FAT	11	6	GRAMS
TOTAL CHOLESTEROL	42	23	MILLIGRAMS
TOTAL SODIUM	3354	2236	MILLIGRAMS
TOTAL FIBRE	8	5	GRAMS
% CALORIES FROM FAT	16	16	

Jalapeño Cheese Bread

For best results, use cheddar cheese that's made with jalapeño peppers. Such cheese is available in most supermarkets.

1½-pound

2 teaspoons active dry yeast

1¼ cup grated cheddar/jalapeño cheese

½ teaspoon cilantro (coriander)

3½ teaspoons sugar

½ teaspoon salt

1 teaspoon dry mustard

2½ tablespoons dried minced onion

2½ cups bread flour

7 ounces warm milk

2½ tablespoons butter

1-pound

1½ teaspoons active dry yeast

¾ cup grated cheddar/jalapeño cheese

½ teaspoon cilantro (coriander)

2½ teaspoons sugar

½ teaspoon salt

½ teaspoon dry mustard

1½ tablespoons dried minced onion

1⅔ cups bread flour

4½ ounces warm milk

1½ tablespoons butter

Note:

For machines with yeast dispensers, use 4 teaspoons of yeast for the 1½-pound loaf.

NUTRITIONAL ANALYSIS			
	1½-POUND	1-POUND	
TOTAL CALORIES	2262	1453	
TOTAL PROTEIN	87	56	GRAMS
TOTAL CARBOHYDRATES	287	191	GRAMS
TOTAL FAT	84	51	GRAMS
TOTAL SATURATED FAT	50	30	GRAMS
TOTAL CHOLESTEROL	235	141	MILLIGRAMS
TOTAL SODIUM	2062	1669	MILLIGRAMS
TOTAL FIBRE	6	4	GRAMS
% CALORIES FROM FAT	34	32	

Nut Bread

Nut bread is excellent with all kinds of cheese.

1½-pound

1½ teaspoons active dry yeast

2¼ cups + 2 tablespoons bread flour

½ cup chopped or ground nuts

½ cup brown sugar

½ cup warm milk

1 egg

½ teaspoon walnut or almond extract

½ teaspoon vanilla extract

2½ tablespoons butter

¼ cup warm water

1 teaspoon salt

1½ teaspoons cinnamon

1-pound

1 teaspoon active dry yeast

1½ cups + 2 tablespoons bread flour

⅓ cup chopped or ground nuts

⅓ cup brown sugar

2½ ounces warm milk

1 egg

½ teaspoon walnut or almond extract

½ teaspoon vanilla extract

1½ tablespoons butter

1½ ounces warm water

½ teaspoon salt

1 teaspoon cinnamon

Notes:
1. For machines with yeast dispensers, use 3 teaspoons of yeast for the 1½-pound loaf.
2. Measure the nuts whole before chopping or grinding them.

	NUTRITIONAL ANALYSIS		
	1½-POUND	1-POUND	
TOTAL CALORIES	2365	1602	
TOTAL PROTEIN	60	42	GRAMS
TOTAL CARBOHYDRATES	362	244	GRAMS
TOTAL FAT	78	51	GRAMS
TOTAL SATURATED FAT	24	15	GRAMS
TOTAL CHOLESTEROL	296	263	MILLIGRAMS
TOTAL SODIUM	172	133	MILLIGRAMS
TOTAL FIBRE	8	6	GRAMS
% CALORIES FROM FAT	29	29	

Olive Bread

This bread has the flavor of olives and it has small olive pieces throughout the loaf.

1½-pound

1 teaspoon active dry yeast

5 tablespoons chopped black olives

3 cups + 1 tablespoon bread flour

1 teaspoon salt

2 tablespoons sugar

2 tablespoons olive oil

9 ounces warm water

1-pound

½ teaspoon active dry yeast

3½ tablespoons chopped black olives

2 cups bread flour

½ teaspoon salt

1½ tablespoons sugar

1 tablespoon olive oil

¾ cup warm water

Note:

For machines with yeast dispensers, use 2 teaspoons of yeast for the 1½-pound loaf.

NUTRITIONAL ANALYSIS			
	1½-POUND	1-POUND	
TOTAL CALORIES	1897	1212	
TOTAL PROTEIN	52	34	GRAMS
TOTAL CARBOHYDRATES	332	219	GRAMS
TOTAL FAT	38	21	GRAMS
TOTAL SATURATED FAT	5	3	GRAMS
TOTAL CHOLESTEROL	0	0	
SODIUM	2513	1332	MILLIGRAMS
TOTAL FIBRE	8	5	GRAMS
% CALORIES FROM FAT	18	16	

Potato Sesame Bread

The soft texture from the potato flakes combined with the nutty flavor of the sesame seeds make this an excellent breakfast bread.

1½-pound

1 teaspoon active dry yeast

2¾ cups bread flour

1 teaspoon parsley flakes

3 tablespoons sesame seeds

1 teaspoon salt

4 tablespoons instant mashed-potato flakes or buds

¼ cup instant dry milk

2 tablespoons sugar

½ cup buttermilk

2 eggs

2 tablespoons butter

5 ounces warm water

1-pound

½ teaspoon active dry yeast

1¾ cups + 2 tablespoons bread flour

½ teaspoon parsley flakes

2 tablespoons sesame seeds

½ teaspoon salt

3 tablespoons instant mashed-potato flakes or buds

3 tablespoons instant dry milk

1½ tablespoons sugar

2½ ounces buttermilk

1 egg

1½ tablespoons butter

3½ ounces warm water

Note:

For machines with yeast dispensers, use 2 teaspoons of yeast for the 1½-pound loaf.

NUTRITIONAL ANALYSIS			
	1½-POUND	1-POUND	
TOTAL CALORIES	2171	1473	
TOTAL PROTEIN	78	51	GRAMS
TOTAL CARBOHYDRATES	333	229	GRAMS
TOTAL FAT	57	38	GRAMS
TOTAL SATURATED FAT	21	14	GRAMS
TOTAL CHOLESTEROL	503	269	MILLIGRAMS
TOTAL SODIUM	2652	1414	MILLIGRAMS
TOTAL FIBRE	7	5	GRAMS
% CALORIES FROM FAT	24	23	

Raisin Walnut Bread

This white bread has whole-grain flavor. If you like it sweeter, try doubling the sugar in the recipe.

1½-pound

2 teaspoons active dry yeast

2¼ cups bread flour

¼ cup chopped walnuts

¼ cup golden raisins

⅓ cup whole-wheat flour

2 tablespoons oat bran

⅓ cup rye flour

1 teaspoon salt

1½ teaspoons sugar

½ teaspoon walnut extract

1 cup warm water

1-pound

1½ teaspoons active dry yeast

1½ cups bread flour

2 tablespoons chopped walnuts

2 tablespoons golden raisins

¼ cup whole-wheat flour

1½ tablespoons oat bran

¼ cup rye flour

½ teaspoon salt

1 teaspoon sugar

¼ teaspoon walnut extract

6½ ounces warm water

Note:

For machines with yeast dispensers, use 3½ teaspoons of yeast for the 1½-pound loaf.

NUTRITIONAL ANALYSIS			
	1½-POUND	1-POUND	
TOTAL CALORIES	1740	1137	
TOTAL PROTEIN	55	37	GRAMS
TOTAL CARBOHYDRATES	327	218	GRAMS
TOTAL FAT	26	15	GRAMS
TOTAL SATURATED FAT	3	2	GRAMS
TOTAL CHOLESTEROL	0	0	
TOTAL SODIUM	2148	1076	MILLIGRAMS
TOTAL FIBRE	20	14	GRAMS
% CALORIES FROM FAT	14	12	

Shredded-Wheat Nut Bread

The small amount of shredded-wheat cereal in this bread gives it a light but distinct wheat flavor, although it retains the texture and appearance of white bread.

1½-pound

1 teaspoon active dry yeast

3 cups bread flour

¼ cup chopped nuts

1 shredded-wheat biscuit

½ teaspoon salt

1 tablespoon molasses

½ tablespoon olive oil

¾ cup warm milk

¼ cup warm water

1-pound

½ teaspoon active dry yeast

2 cups bread flour

3 tablespoons chopped nuts

⅔ shredded-wheat biscuit

¼ teaspoon salt

½ tablespoon molasses

½ tablespoon olive oil

½ cup warm milk

1½ ounces warm water

Note:

For machines with yeast dispensers, use 2 teaspoons of yeast for the 1½ pound loaf.

NUTRITIONAL ANALYSIS			
	1½-POUND	1-POUND	
TOTAL CALORIES	1939	1323	
TOTAL PROTEIN	62	42	GRAMS
TOTAL CARBOHYDRATES	340	226	GRAMS
TOTAL FAT	35	27	GRAMS
TOTAL SATURATED FAT	5	4	GRAMS
TOTAL CHOLESTEROL	8	5	MILLIGRAMS
TOTAL SODIUM	1184	609	MILLIGRAMS
TOTAL FIBRE	8	5	GRAMS
% CALORIES FROM FAT	16	18	

Sunflower Bread

This nutritious bread has the aroma and flavor of sunflower seeds. The sunflower-seed oil, released during baking, permeates the bread, giving it a distinctively nutty taste.

1½-pound

1½ teaspoons active dry yeast

2½ cups bread flour

4 tablespoons sunflower seeds

1½ teaspoons salt

½ cup oat bran

1 tablespoon sugar

2 tablespoons molasses

2 tablespoons butter

½ cup warm milk

4½ ounces warm water

1-pound

1 teaspoon active dry yeast

1¾ cups bread flour

2½ tablespoons sunflower seeds

1 teaspoon salt

⅓ cup oat bran

2 teaspoons sugar

1½ tablespoons molasses

1 tablespoon butter

3 ounces warm milk

3 ounces warm water

Note:

For machines with yeast dispensers, use 3 teaspoons of yeast for the 1½-pound loaf.

NUTRITIONAL ANALYSIS			
	1½-POUND	1-POUND	
TOTAL CALORIES	1979	1310	
TOTAL PROTEIN	60	41	GRAMS
TOTAL CARBOHYDRATES	327	224	GRAMS
TOTAL FAT	49	28	GRAMS
TOTAL SATURATED FAT	18	10	GRAMS
TOTAL CHOLESTEROL	67	35	MILLIGRAMS
TOTAL SODIUM	3299	2207	MILLIGRAMS
TOTAL FIBRE	12	8	GRAMS
% CALORIES FROM FAT	22	20	

Walnut Bread

This bread has a great walnut flavor and crunch. It's excellent toasted with cheese.

1½-pound

2 teaspoons active dry yeast

2 cups bread flour

¾ cup chopped walnuts

1 teaspoon salt

3 tablespoons brown sugar

1 cup whole-wheat flour

½ teaspoon walnut extract

5 ounces warm milk

½ cup warm water

1-pound

1½ teaspoons active dry yeast

1⅓ cups bread flour

½ cup chopped walnuts

½ teaspoon salt

2 tablespoons brown sugar

⅔ cup whole-wheat flour

¼ teaspoon walnut extract

3 ounces warm milk

3 ounces warm water

Note:

For machines with yeast dispensers, use 3½ teaspoons of yeast for the 1½-pound loaf.

NUTRITIONAL ANALYSIS			
	1½-POUND	1-POUND	
TOTAL CALORIES	2205	1467	
TOTAL PROTEIN	69	46	GRAMS
TOTAL CARBOHYDRATES	351	234	GRAMS
TOTAL FAT	64	43	GRAMS
TOTAL SATURATED FAT	7	5	GRAMS
TOTAL CHOLESTEROL	6	4	MILLIGRAMS
TOTAL SODIUM	2237	1131	MILLIGRAMS
TOTAL FIBRE	24	16	GRAMS
% CALORIES FROM FAT	26	26	

Walnut Herb Bread

This bread has a spicy flavor in addition to the light walnut taste and crunch. You could substitute almonds, Brazil nuts, or pecans for walnuts.

1½-pound	1-pound
1½ teaspoons active dry yeast	1 teaspoon active dry yeast
3 cups bread flour	2 cups bread flour
¼ cup chopped walnuts	2 tablespoons chopped walnuts
½ teaspoon dill weed	¼ teaspoon dill weed
½ teaspoon oregano	¼ teaspoon oregano
½ teaspoon dried parsley flakes	¼ teaspoon dried parsley flakes
½ teaspoon dried lemon peel	¼ teaspoon dried lemon peel
1½ teaspoons salt	1 teaspoon salt
1 tablespoon brown sugar	2 teaspoons brown sugar
1½ tablespoons butter	1 tablespoon butter
9 ounces warm water	¾ cup warm water

Notes:

1. For machines with yeast dispensers, use 3 teaspoons of yeast for the 1½-pound loaf.
2. If salted nuts are used, reduce the salt by ½ teaspoon.

NUTRITIONAL ANALYSIS			
	1½-POUND	1-POUND	
TOTAL CALORIES	1893	1229	
TOTAL PROTEIN	55	36	GRAMS
TOTAL CARBOHYDRATES	319	212	GRAMS
TOTAL FAT	43	25	GRAMS
TOTAL SATURATED FAT	13	9	GRAMS
TOTAL CHOLESTEROL	47	31	MILLIGRAMS
TOTAL SODIUM	3215	2143	MILLIGRAMS
TOTAL FIBRE	8	5	GRAMS
% CALORIES FROM FAT	20	19	

Wheat-Germ Bread

The addition of nutritious wheat germ gives this traditional white bread a slightly nutty flavor.

1½-pound

1½ teaspoons active dry yeast

2¾ cups bread flour

½ cup wheat germ

2 teaspoons salt

3 tablespoons olive oil

2 tablespoons honey

1 cup warm water

1-pound

1 teaspoon active dry yeast

1¾ cups bread flour

¼ cup wheat germ

1½ teaspoons salt

2 tablespoons olive oil

1 tablespoon honey

5 ounces warm water

Note:

For machines with yeast dispensers, use 3 teaspoons of yeast for the 1½-pound loaf.

NUTRITIONAL ANALYSIS			
	1½-POUND	1-POUND	
TOTAL CALORIES	2057	1275	
TOTAL PROTEIN	65	39	GRAMS
TOTAL CARBOHYDRATES	340	207	GRAMS
TOTAL FAT	54	35	GRAMS
TOTAL SATURATED FAT	7	5	GRAMS
TOTAL CHOLESTEROL	0	0	
TOTAL SODIUM	4275	3205	MILLIGRAMS
TOTAL FIBRE	13	7	GRAMS
% CALORIES FROM FAT	24	25	

WHEAT BREADS

This section features breads that emphasize whole wheat, both in flavor and texture. The breads vary in the percentage of whole-wheat flour used, but each is unique in its distinctive wheat flavor combined with the flavors of other wonderful ingredients.

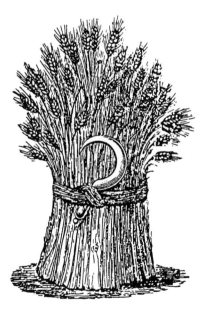

Bran Bread

Here, oat bran combines with wheat to make a soft, light wheat bread that slices like white bread but has a unique wheat flavor.

1½-pound

2 teaspoons active dry yeast

1¼ cups bread flour

1¼ cups whole-wheat flour

¾ cup oat bran

1½ teaspoons salt

3 tablespoons brown sugar

3 tablespoons butter

9 ounces warm water

1-pound

1½ teaspoons active dry yeast

¾ cup + 2 tablespoons bread flour

¾ cup + 2 tablespoons whole-wheat flour

½ cup oat bran

1 teaspoon salt

2 tablespoons brown sugar

2 tablespoons butter

6 ounces warm water

Notes:

1. For machines with yeast dispensers, use 3½ teaspoons of yeast for the 1½-pound loaf.
2. For a variation, try using wheat bran instead of oat bran.

NUTRITIONAL ANALYSIS			
	1½-POUND	1-POUND	
TOTAL CALORIES	1802	1199	
TOTAL PROTEIN	56	37	GRAMS
TOTAL CARBOHYDRATES	312	208	GRAMS
TOTAL FAT	45	30	GRAMS
TOTAL SATURATED FAT	23	15	GRAMS
TOTAL CHOLESTEROL	93	62	MILLIGRAMS
TOTAL SODIUM	3222	2148	MILLIGRAMS
TOTAL FIBRE	32	21	GRAMS
% CALORIES FROM FAT	22	22	

Cashew Date Bread

This bread was created for cashew-nut lovers. The dates give the bread an exotic and sweet flavor that nicely complements that of the cashew nuts.

1½-pound

1½ teaspoons active dry yeast

2 cups bread flour

¼ cup chopped dates

¼ cup chopped raw cashew nuts

½ cup whole-wheat flour

½ teaspoon cinnamon

1 teaspoon salt

3 tablespoons rolled oats

2 tablespoons butter

3 tablespoons honey

3 ounces warm buttermilk

¾ cup warm water

1-pound

1 teaspoon active dry yeast

1⅓ cups bread flour

3 tablespoons chopped dates

3 tablespoons chopped raw cashew nuts

⅓ cup whole-wheat flour

¼ teaspoon cinnamon

½ teaspoon salt

2 tablespoons rolled oats

1½ tablespoons butter

2 tablespoons honey

2 ounces warm buttermilk

½ cup warm water

Notes:

1. For machines with yeast dispensers, use 3 teaspoons of yeast for the 1½-pound loaf.
2. If roasted, salted cashews are used, reduce the salt by ¼ teaspoon.

NUTRITIONAL ANALYSIS			
	1½-POUND	1-POUND	
TOTAL CALORIES	2004	1375	
TOTAL PROTEIN	54	36	GRAMS
TOTAL CARBOHYDRATES	346	233	GRAMS
TOTAL FAT	49	36	GRAMS
TOTAL SATURATED FAT	17	13	GRAMS
TOTAL CHOLESTEROL	70	52	MILLIGRAMS
TOTAL SODIUM	2204	1115	MILLIGRAMS
TOTAL FIBRE	18	12	GRAMS
% CALORIES FROM FAT	22	24	

Date Molasses Bread

Dates, molasses, and a high percentage of whole-wheat flour make this slightly sweet bread a favorite for toast.

1½-pound

2 teaspoons active dry yeast

½ cup bread flour

2½ cups whole-wheat flour

¾ cup chopped dates

½ teaspoon salt

1 tablespoon butter

½ cup warm milk

2 tablespoons molasses

5 ounces warm water

1-pound

1½ teaspoons active dry yeast

⅓ cup bread flour

1⅔ cups whole-wheat flour

½ cup chopped dates

½ teaspoon salt

½ tablespoon butter

3 ounces warm milk

1½ tablespoons molasses

3½ ounces warm water

Notes:

1. For machines with yeast dispensers, use 4 teaspoons of yeast for the 1½-pound loaf.
2. If your machine is equipped with a whole-grain cycle, use it for this bread.
3. You may add the dates at the mix-cycle beep, if your machine is so equipped.

NUTRITIONAL ANALYSIS			
	1½-POUND	1-POUND	
TOTAL CALORIES	1918	1277	
TOTAL PROTEIN	58	39	GRAMS
TOTAL CARBOHYDRATES	401	270	GRAMS
TOTAL FAT	20	12	GRAMS
TOTAL SATURATED FAT	9	5	GRAMS
TOTAL CHOLESTEROL	36	19	MILLIGRAMS
TOTAL SODIUM	1169	1142	MILLIGRAMS
TOTAL FIBRE	46	31	GRAMS
% CALORIES FROM FAT	9	8	

Farmer's Bread

This is a traditional, crumbly-textured whole-wheat bread. Dough conditioner (optional) can be added to give the bread a less crumbly texture, if desired.

1½-pound

1½ teaspoons active dry yeast

1 cup bread flour

½ cup seedless raisins

1 tablespoon dough conditioner (optional)

2 cups whole-wheat flour

1 teaspoon salt

1½ tablespoons brown sugar

1½ tablespoons butter

9 ounces warm milk

1-pound

1 teaspoon active dry yeast

¾ cup bread flour

⅓ cup seedless raisins

2 teaspoons dough conditioner (optional)

1¼ cups whole-wheat flour

½ teaspoon salt

1 tablespoon brown sugar

1 tablespoon butter

¾ cup warm milk

Notes:

1. For machines with yeast dispensers, use 3 teaspoons of yeast for the 1½-pound loaf.
2. If your machine is equipped with a whole-grain cycle, use it for this bread.

NUTRITIONAL ANALYSIS			
	1½-POUND	1-POUND	
TOTAL CALORIES	1878	1258	
TOTAL PROTEIN	62	41	GRAMS
TOTAL CARBOHYDRATES	365	244	GRAMS
TOTAL FAT	27	18	GRAMS
TOTAL SATURATED FAT	14	9	GRAMS
TOTAL CHOLESTEROL	58	39	MILLIGRAMS
TOTAL SODIUM	2293	1173	MILLIGRAMS
TOTAL FIBRE	37	23	GRAMS
% CALORIES FROM FAT	13	13	

Graham Bread

Graham flour's special milling process gives it taste that's slightly sweeter than regular whole-wheat flour. That sweetness is evident in this light wheat bread.

1½-pound

1 teaspoon active dry yeast

2¼ cups + 3 tablespoons bread flour

¾ cup graham flour

1 teaspoon salt

⅓ cup dry milk

3 tablespoons brown sugar

1 egg

1½ tablespoons molasses

1½ tablespoons butter

1 cup warm water

1-pound

½ teaspoon active dry yeast

1½ cups + 2 tablespoons bread flour

½ cup graham flour

½ teaspoon salt

¼ cup dry milk

2 tablespoons brown sugar

1 egg

1 tablespoon molasses

1 tablespoon butter

5 ounces warm water

Notes:

1. For machines with yeast dispensers, use 2 teaspoons of yeast for the 1½-pound loaf.
2. You may substitute whole-wheat flour for graham flour, if graham flour isn't available.

NUTRITIONAL ANALYSIS			
	1½-POUND	1-POUND	
TOTAL CALORIES	2094	1430	
TOTAL PROTEIN	70	50	GRAMS
TOTAL CARBOHYDRATES	386	259	GRAMS
TOTAL FAT	30	21	GRAMS
TOTAL SATURATED FAT	13	9	GRAMS
TOTAL CHOLESTEROL	265	248	MILLIGRAMS
TOTAL SODIUM	2403	1282	MILLIGRAMS
TOTAL FIBRE	17	11	GRAMS
% CALORIES FROM FAT	13	14	

Honey Wheat Bread

This traditional light wheat bread has the texture of white bread and a mild wheat taste.

1½-pound

1½ teaspoons active dry yeast

½ teaspoon sugar

2 cups bread flour

1½ teaspoons salt

1¼ cups whole-wheat flour

1 egg

1½ tablespoons butter

4 tablespoons honey

½ cup warm milk

¼ cup warm water

1-pound

1 teaspoon active dry yeast

½ teaspoon sugar

1¼ cups bread flour

1 teaspoon salt

¾ cup whole-wheat flour

1 egg

1 tablespoon butter

2 tablespoons honey

¼ cup warm milk

¼ cup warm water

Note:

For machines with yeast dispensers, use 3 teaspoons of yeast for the 1½-pound loaf.

NUTRITIONAL ANALYSIS			
	1½-POUND	1-POUND	
TOTAL CALORIES	2033	1259	
TOTAL PROTEIN	65	42	GRAMS
TOTAL CARBOHYDRATES	381	228	GRAMS
TOTAL FAT	31	22	GRAMS
TOTAL SATURATED FAT	14	10	GRAMS
TOTAL CHOLESTEROL	265	247	MILLIGRAMS
TOTAL SODIUM	3331	2231	MILLIGRAMS
TOTAL FIBRE	23	14	GRAMS
% CALORIES FROM FAT	14	15	

Sesame Wheat Bread

This light wheat bread has a nutty sesame flavor. Try varying the amount of sesame seeds to suit your taste.

1½-pound

2 teaspoons active dry yeast

2¼ cups bread flour

¾ cup whole-wheat flour

1 tablespoon sesame seeds

1½ teaspoons salt

1 tablespoon brown sugar

2 tablespoons butter

3 ounces warm milk

¾ cup warm water

1-pound

1½ teaspoon active dry yeast

1½ cups bread flour

½ cup whole-wheat flour

2 teaspoons sesame seeds

1 teaspoon salt

2 teaspoons brown sugar

1½ tablespoons butter

¼ cup warm milk

½ cup warm water

Note:

For machines with yeast dispensers, use 3½ teaspoons of yeast for the 1½-pound loaf.

NUTRITIONAL ANALYSIS			
	1½-POUND	1-POUND	
TOTAL CALORIES	1774	1201	
TOTAL PROTEIN	56	38	GRAMS
TOTAL CARBOHYDRATES	311	207	GRAMS
TOTAL FAT	35	25	GRAMS
TOTAL SATURATED FAT	16	12	GRAMS
TOTAL CHOLESTEROL	66	49	MILLIGRAMS
TOTAL SODIUM	3259	2173	MILLIGRAMS
TOTAL FIBRE	17	11	GRAMS
% CALORIES FROM FAT	18	19	

Sunflower Potato Bread

The mixture of potato flakes, sunflower seeds, and wheat gives this bread its hearty, whole-grain flavor.

1½-pound

2 teaspoons active dry yeast

3 tablespoons brown sugar

2 cups bread flour

3 tablespoons sunflower seeds

1 cup whole-wheat flour

1½ teaspoons salt

½ cup instant mashed-potato flakes or buds

3 tablespoons butter

1¼ cups warm water

1-pound

1½ teaspoons active dry yeast

2 tablespoons brown sugar

1⅓ cups bread flour

2 tablespoons sunflower seeds

⅔ cup whole-wheat flour

1 teaspoon salt

⅓ cup instant mashed-potato flakes or buds

2 tablespoons butter

7 ounces warm water

Note:

For machines with yeast dispensers, use 3½ teaspoons of yeast for the 1½-pound loaf.

NUTRITIONAL ANALYSIS			
	1½-POUND	1-POUND	
TOTAL CALORIES	2134	1422	
TOTAL PROTEIN	59	40	GRAMS
TOTAL CARBOHYDRATES	350	234	GRAMS
TOTAL FAT	59	39	GRAMS
TOTAL SATURATED FAT	24	16	GRAMS
TOTAL CHOLESTEROL	93	62	MILLIGRAMS
TOTAL SODIUM	3581	2385	MILLIGRAMS
TOTAL FIBRE	20	14	GRAMS
% CALORIES FROM FAT	25	25	

Whole-Wheat & Buckwheat Bread

This bread doesn't rise much, usually making a dense, flat loaf. If you like buckwheat, this is an excellent, densely textured bread.

1½-pound

2½ teaspoons active dry yeast

1 cup buckwheat flour

2 cups whole-wheat flour

1½ tablespoons wheat glutten (optional)

2 teaspoons salt

1 tablespoon brown sugar

2 tablespoons butter

1½ tablespoons molasses

¼ cup warm water

¾ cup warm milk

1-pound

2 teaspoons active dry yeast

⅔ cup buckwheat flour

1⅓ cups whole-wheat flour

1 tablespoon wheat gluten (optional)

1 teaspoon salt

2 teaspoons brown sugar

1½ tablespoons butter

1 tablespoon molasses

1½ ounces warm water

½ cup warm milk

Notes:

1. For machines with yeast dispensers, use 4½ teaspoons of yeast for the 1½-pound loaf.
2. For machines with low-power motors, add 2 tablespoons of warm water for the 1½-pound loaf.
3. If your machine is equipped with a whole-grain cycle, use it for this bread.

NUTRITIONAL ANALYSIS			
	1½-POUND	1-POUND	
TOTAL CALORIES	1651	1120	
TOTAL PROTEIN	57	38	GRAMS
TOTAL CARBOHYDRATES	304	203	GRAMS
TOTAL FAT	33	24	GRAMS
TOTAL SATURATED FAT	17	13	GRAMS
TOTAL CHOLESTEROL	70	52	MILLIGRAMS
TOTAL SODIUM	4390	2217	MILLIGRAMS
TOTAL FIBRE	31	21	GRAMS
% CALORIES FROM FAT	18	19	

Whole-Wheat Buttermilk Raisin Bread

This coarsely textured wheat bread has a slightly sweet taste. Add additional raisins, if you like.

1½-pound

2 teaspoons active dry yeast

½ cup bread flour

2½ cups whole-wheat flour

6 tablespoons raisins

½ teaspoon baking soda

1½ teaspoons salt

2½ tablespoons butter

5 ounces buttermilk

2 tablespoons honey

¼ cup warm water

1-pound

1½ teaspoons active dry yeast

½ cup bread flour

1½ cups whole-wheat flour

¼ cup raisins

¼ teaspoon baking soda

1 teaspoon salt

1½ tablespoons butter

½ cup buttermilk

1½ tablespoons honey

2 tablespoons warm water

Notes:

1. For machines with yeast dispensers, use 3½ teaspoons of yeast for the 1½-pound loaf.
2. If your machine is equipped with a whole-grain cycle, use it for this bread.

	NUTRITIONAL ANALYSIS		
	1½-POUND	1-POUND	
TOTAL CALORIES	1884	1275	
TOTAL PROTEIN	60	41	GRAMS
TOTAL CARBOHYDRATES	353	242	GRAMS
TOTAL FAT	37	23	GRAMS
TOTAL SATURATED FAT	20	12	GRAMS
TOTAL CHOLESTEROL	90	57	GRAMS
TOTAL SODIUM	3310	2220	MILLIGRAMS
TOTAL FIBRE	42	26	GRAMS
% CALORIES FROM FAT	18	16	

Whole-Wheat Cranberry Bread

Tart cranberries give this 100 percent–wheat bread a tangy flavor. It has a crumbly whole-wheat texture, which makes it excellent for toast.

1½-pound

2 teaspoons active dry yeast

3½ cups whole-wheat flour

½ cup whole cranberries

½ cup brown sugar

1½ teaspoons salt

3 tablespoons molasses

2 tablespoons butter

¾ cup warm water

1-pound

1½ teaspoons active dry yeast

2¼ cups + 2 tablespoons whole-wheat flour

⅓ cup whole cranberries

⅓ cup brown sugar

1 teaspoon salt

2 tablespoons molasses

1½ tablespoons butter

½ cup warm water

Notes:

1. For machines with yeast dispensers, use 3½ teaspoons of yeast for the 1½-pound loaf.
2. If your machine is equipped with a whole-grain cycle, use it for this bread.

NUTRITIONAL ANALYSIS			
	1½-POUND	1-POUND	
TOTAL CALORIES	2317	1576	
TOTAL PROTEIN	60	41	GRAMS
TOTAL CARBOHYDRATES	477	321	GRAMS
TOTAL FAT	31	22	GRAMS
TOTAL SATURATED FAT	16	12	GRAMS
TOTAL CHOLESTEROL	62	47	MILLIGRAMS
TOTAL SODIUM	3303	2202	MILLIGRAMS
TOTAL FIBRE	54	36	GRAMS
% CALORIES FROM FAT	12	13	

Whole-Wheat Egg Bread

This 100-percent wheat bread has a soft texture due to the eggs. Using maple syrup as a sweetener takes the edge off the sometimes slightly bitter taste of the whole wheat.

1½-pound

3 teaspoons active dry yeast

1 teaspoon sugar

3¼ cups whole-wheat flour

2 teaspoons salt

3 eggs

4 tablespoons olive oil

4 tablespoons maple syrup

3 ounces warm water

1-pound

2 teaspoons active dry yeast

½ teaspoon sugar

2¼ cups whole-wheat flour

1 teaspoon salt

2 eggs

2½ tablespoons olive oil

2½ tablespoons maple syrup

¼ cup warm water

Notes:

1. For machines with yeast dispensers, use 5½ teaspoons of yeast for the 1½-pound loaf.
2. If your machine is equipped with a whole-grain cycle, use it for this bread.
3. Because eggs vary in their effect on the consistency of the dough, be sure to watch the dough as it mixes. If it seems too runny, add flour, one tablespoon at a time, until the consistency is about right.

NUTRITIONAL ANALYSIS			
	1½-POUND	1-POUND	
TOTAL CALORIES	2260	1510	
TOTAL PROTEIN	75	52	GRAMS
TOTAL CARBOHYDRATES	344	233	GRAMS
TOTAL FAT	76	49	GRAMS
TOTAL SATURATED FAT	13	9	GRAMS
TOTAL CHOLESTEROL	639	426	MILLIGRAMS
TOTAL SODIUM	4500	2288	MILLIGRAMS
TOTAL FIBRE	50	35	GRAMS
% CALORIES FROM FAT	30	29	

Whole-Wheat Potato Bread

If you like soft-textured whole-wheat bread, try this. The potato flakes soften the bread and give it a spongy texture.

1½-pound

2 teaspoons active dry yeast

2¼ cups whole-wheat flour

1 teaspoon cardamom

3 tablespoons nonfat dry milk

2 teaspoons salt

5 tablespoons instant mashed-potato flakes or buds

5 tablespoons brown sugar

1 egg

4 tablespoons butter

7 ounces warm water

1-pound

1½ teaspoons active dry yeast

1¾ cups whole-wheat flour

½ teaspoon cardamom

2 tablespoons nonfat dry milk

1½ teaspoons salt

3½ tablespoons instant mashed-potato flakes or buds

3½ tablespoons brown sugar

1 egg

2½ tablespoons butter

5 ounces warm water

Notes:

1. For machines with yeast dispensers, use 3½ teaspoons of yeast for the 1½-pound loaf.
2. If your machine is equipped with a whole-grain cycle, use it for this bread.

NUTRITIONAL ANALYSIS			
	1½-POUND	1-POUND	
TOTAL CALORIES	1802	1324	
TOTAL PROTEIN	53	42	GRAMS
TOTAL CARBOHYDRATES	284	214	GRAMS
TOTAL FAT	60	40	GRAMS
TOTAL SATURATED FAT	31	20	GRAMS
TOTAL CHOLESTEROL	340	293	MILLIGRAMS
TOTALSODIUM	4674	3501	MILLIGRAMS
TOTAL FIBRE	35	27	GRAMS
% CALORIES FROM FAT	30	27	

Whole-Wheat Sally Lunn Bread

Because of its sweet flavor and whole-grain richness, this was my tasters' favorite 100-percent whole-wheat bread.

1½-pound	1-pound
2 teaspoons active dry yeast	1½ teaspoons active dry yeast
¼ teaspoon cream of tartar	¼ teaspoon cream of tartar
1 teaspoon cardamom	½ teaspoon cardamom
3¼ cups whole-wheat flour	2 cups + 2 tablespoons whole-wheat flour
1 teaspoon salt	½ teaspoon salt
½ cup + 1 tablespoon brown sugar	6 tablespoons brown sugar
2 eggs	1 egg
4 tablespoons butter	2½ tablespoons butter
7 ounces warm milk	5 ounces warm milk

Notes:

1. For machines with yeast dispensers, use 3½ teaspoons of yeast for the 1½-pound loaf.
2. If your machine is equipped with a whole-grain cycle, use it for this bread.

NUTRITIONAL ANALYSIS			
	1½-POUND	1-POUND	
TOTAL CALORIES	2435	1570	
TOTAL PROTEIN	75	48	GRAMS
TOTAL CARBOHYDRATES	416	274	GRAMS
TOTAL FAT	65	40	GRAMS
TOTAL SATURATED FAT	34	21	GRAMS
TOTAL CHOLESTEROL	559	297	MILLIGRAMS
TOTAL SODIUM	2411	1236	MILLIGRAMS
TOTAL FIBRE	50	33	GRAMS
% CALORIES FROM FAT	24	23	

Whole-Wheat Sourdough Bread

If you like both sourdough bread and wheat bread, try this. Sourdough adds a pungent flavor to this wheat bread. It's excellent topped with butter and honey.

1½-pound

1½ teaspoons active dry yeast

1 cup bread flour

1 teaspoon salt

2 cups whole-wheat flour

¾ cup sourdough starter

1 cup warm water

2 tablespoons honey

1-pound

1 teaspoon active dry yeast

½ cup bread flour

½ teaspoon salt

1⅓ cups whole-wheat flour

½ cup sourdough starter

5 ounces warm water

1½ tablespoons honey

Notes:

1. For machines with yeast dispensers, use 3 teaspoons of yeast for the 1½-pound loaf.
2. If you don't have sourdough starter, you can make your own. See pages 31–33.
3. Because sourdough starter varies in consistency, check the dough when mixing. If it seems too runny, add flour, one tablespoon at a time. If it seems too stiff, add warm water, one tablespoon at a time.

	NUTRITIONAL ANALYSIS		
	1½-POUND	1-POUND	
TOTAL CALORIES	1811	1217	
TOTAL PROTEIN	63	42	GRAMS
TOTAL CARBOHYDRATES	382	257	GRAMS
TOTAL FAT	9	6	GRAMS
TOTAL SATURATED FAT	1	1	GRAM
TOTAL CHOLESTEROL	0	0	MILLIGRAMS
TOTAL SODIUM	2139	1071	MILLIGRAMS
TOTAL FIBRE	34	23	GRAMS
% CALORIES FROM FAT	4	4	

Whole-Wheat Sunflower Bread

Since sunflower-seed oil permeates the dough during the mixing and baking processes, this light wheat bread has a nutty flavor. The texture is similar to that of white breads, so it is easily sliced.

1½-pound

1½ teaspoons active dry yeast

4 tablespoons sunflower seeds

1¾ cups bread flour

1¼ cups whole-wheat flour

1½ teaspoons salt

2 tablespoons brown sugar

1½ tablespoons butter

9 ounces warm water

1-pound

1 teaspoon active dry yeast

2½ tablespoons sunflower seeds

1¼ cups bread flour

¾ cup whole-wheat flour

1 teaspoon salt

1½ tablespoons brown sugar

1 tablespoon butter

¾ cup warm water

Note:

For machines with yeast dispensers, use 3 teaspoons of yeast for the 1½-pound loaf.

NUTRITIONAL ANALYSIS			
	1½-POUND	1-POUND	
TOTAL CALORIES	1824	1143	
TOTAL PROTEIN	57	35	GRAMS
TOTAL CARBOHYDRATES	318	198	GRAMS
TOTAL FAT	40	28	GRAMS
TOTAL SATURATED FAT	13	15	GRAMS
TOTAL CHOLESTEROL	47	62	MILLIGRAMS
TOTAL SODIUM	3215	1074	MILLIGRAMS
TOTAL FIBRE	24	25	GRAMS
% CALORIES FROM FAT	20	22	

RYE BREADS

The distinctive taste of rye bread is loved the world over. Featured in this section are interesting variations on "standard" rye breads. As you bake rye breads in your bread machine, remember that the dough ball will usually be somewhat stiff and that rye breads don't rise much, giving them their uniquely dense texture.

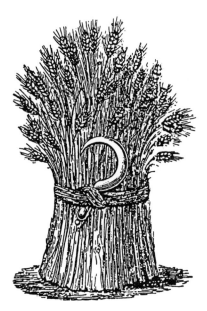

Buckwheat Rye Bread

Due to the small amount of wheat flour used, this bread doesn't rise much. The result, however, is a bread with a dense texture and strong buckwheat flavor that will please buckwheat lovers.

1½-pound

2 teaspoons active dry yeast

1½ tablespoons gluten powder

1 tablespoon brown sugar

1½ cups rye flour

¼ teaspoon ground cloves

1 cup whole-wheat flour

½ cup buckwheat flour

1 teaspoon salt

3 tablespoons molasses

2 tablespoons butter

1 cup + 2 tablespoons warm water

1-pound

1½ teaspoons active dry yeast

1 tablespoon gluten powder

½ tablespoon brown sugar

1 cup rye flour

⅛ teaspoon ground cloves

⅔ cup whole-wheat flour

⅓ cup buckwheat flour

½ teaspoon salt

2 tablespoons molasses

1 tablespoon butter

¾ cup warm water

Notes:

1. For machines with yeast dispensers, use 4 teaspoons of yeast for the 1½-pound loaf.
2. If your machine is equipped with a whole-grain cycle, use it for this bread.

NUTRITIONAL ANALYSIS			
	1½-POUND	1-POUND	
TOTAL CALORIES	1670	1072	
TOTAL PROTEIN	52	35	GRAMS
TOTAL CARBOHYDRATES	312	206	GRAMS
TOTAL FAT	31	17	GRAMS
TOTAL SATURATED FAT	15	8	GRAMS
TOTAL CHOLESTEROL	62	31	MILLIGRAMS
TOTAL SODIUM	2192	1105	MILLIGRAMS
TOTAL FIBRE	39	26	GRAMS
% CALORIES FROM FAT	16	14	

Dijon Rye Bread

This mild rye has a tangy flavor. It's densely textured and doesn't rise much, but it's a great bread for sandwiches. Dijon mustard is made from white wine, vinegar, spices, and ground mustard seed, and it complements the rye flavor quite well.

1½-pound

1½ teaspoons active dry yeast

1 tablespoon gluten powder

2 teaspoons sugar

2¼ cups bread flour

½ cup rye flour

4½ tablespoons oat bran

1½ teaspoons ground caraway seeds

1½ teaspoons salt

4½ tablespoons Dijon mustard

2½ tablespoons molasses

2 tablespoons olive oil

7 ounces warm water

1-pound

1 teaspoon active dry yeast

2 teaspoons gluten powder

1½ teaspoons sugar

1½ cups bread flour

⅓ cup rye flour

3 tablespoons oat bran

1 teaspoon ground caraway seeds

1 teaspoon salt

3 tablespoons Dijon mustard

1½ tablespoons molasses

1½ tablespoons olive oil

4½ ounces warm water

Notes:

1. For machines with yeast dispensers, use 3 teaspoons of yeast for the 1½-pound loaf.
2. For machines with low-power motors, add 2 tablespoons of warm water for the 1½-pound loaf.
3. If your machine is equipped with a whole-grain cycle, use it for this bread.

NUTRITIONAL ANALYSIS			
	1½-POUND	1-POUND	
TOTAL CALORIES	1862	1252	
TOTAL PROTEIN	56	37	GRAMS
TOTAL CARBOHYDRATES	328	216	GRAMS
TOTAL FAT	36	26	GRAMS
TOTAL SATURATED FAT	5	3	GRAMS
TOTAL CHOLESTEROL	0	0	
TOTAL SODIUM	3245	2161	MILLIGRAMS
TOTAL FIBRE	17	11	GRAMS
% CALORIES FROM FAT	17	19	

Dill Rye Bread

This light rye has a spicy flavor. It's excellent as a sandwich bread.

1½-pound

1½ teaspoons active dry yeast

1½ tablespoons brown sugar

½ teaspoon caraway seeds

½ tablespoon dill seeds

2¼ cups bread flour

1 teaspoon salt

½ tablespoon dill weed

4 tablespoons nonfat dry milk

¾ cup rye flour

1½ tablespoons butter

9 ounces warm water

1-pound

1 teaspoon active dry yeast

1 tablespoon brown sugar

½ teaspoon caraway seeds

1 teaspoon dill seeds

1½ cups bread flour

½ teaspoon salt

1 teaspoon dill weed

2½ tablespoons nonfat dry milk

½ cup rye flour

1 tablespoon butter

¾ cup warm water

Notes:

For machines with yeast dispensers, use 3 teaspoons of yeast for the 1½-pound loaf.

NUTRITIONAL ANALYSIS			
	1½-POUND	1-POUND	
TOTAL CALORIES	1720	1144	
TOTAL PROTEIN	55	36	GRAMS
TOTAL CARBOHYDRATES	319	213	GRAMS
TOTAL FAT	25	16	GRAMS
TOTAL SATURATED FAT	12	8	GRAMS
TOTAL CHOLESTEROL	51	34	MILLIGRAMS
TOTAL SODIUM	2276	1157	MILLIGRAMS
TOTAL FIBRE	17	12	GRAMS
% CALORIES FROM FAT	13	13	

Oat Rye Bread

This bread has a soft, but dense, texture and a mild rye flavor. The loaf won't rise much and will stay fairly small.

1½-pound

2 teaspoons active dry yeast

1¼ cups bread flour

1½ teaspoons ground caraway seeds

1½ cups rye flour

¼ cup oat flour

1 teaspoon salt

1 egg

1½ tablespoons butter

1½ tablespoons molasses

6½ ounces warm water

2 teaspoons dough enhancer (optional)

1-pound

1½ teaspoons active dry yeast

¾ cup bread flour

1 teaspoon ground caraway seeds

1 cup rye flour

¼ cup oat flour

½ teaspoon salt

1 egg

1 tablespoon butter

1 tablespoon molases

½ cup warm water

½ tablespoon dough enhancer (optional)

Notes:

1. For machines with yeast dispensers, use 4 teaspoons of yeast for the 1½-pound loaf.
2. If your machine is equipped with a whole-grain cycle, use it for this bread.

NUTRITIONAL ANALYSIS			
	1½-POUND	1-POUND	
TOTAL CALORIES	1600	1085	
TOTAL PROTEIN	48	34	GRAMS
TOTAL CARBOHYDRATES	289	192	GRAMS
TOTAL FAT	29	21	GRAMS
TOTAL SATURATED FAT	13	9	GRAMS
TOTAL CHOLESTEROL	260	244	MILLIGRAMS
TOTAL SODIUM	2229	1152	MILLIGRAMS
TOTAL FIBRE	30	21	GRAMS
% CALORIES FROM FAT	16	17	

Swedish Rye Bread

Fennel seeds and orange juice give this traditional rye bread its distinctive flavor.

1½-pound

1½ teaspoons active dry yeast

2 teaspoons fennel seeds

½ teaspoon sugar

2 cups bread flour

1 cup rye flour

1½ teaspoon salt

1 tablespoon olive oil

4 tablespoons molasses

3 ounces orange juice

3 ounces warm milk

2 tablespoons warm water

1-pound

1 teaspoon active dry yeast

1 teaspoon fennel seeds

½ teaspoon sugar

1⅓ cups bread flour

⅔ cup rye flour

1 teaspoon salt

½ tablespoon olive oil

2½ tablespoons molasses

2 ounces orange juice

2 ounces warm milk

1½ tablespoons warm water

Notes:
1. For machines with yeast dispensers, use 3 teaspoons of yeast for the 1½-pound loaf.
2. For machines with low-power motors, add 2 tablespoons of warm water for the 1½-pound loaf.

NUTRITIONAL ANALYSIS			
	1½-POUND	1-POUND	
TOTAL CALORIES	1808	1178	
TOTAL PROTEIN	48	32	GRAMS
TOTAL CARBOHYDRATES	352	233	GRAMS
TOTAL FAT	21	12	GRAMS
TOTAL SATURATED FAT	3	2	GRAMS
TOTAL CHOLESTEROL	4	3	MILLIGRAMS
TOTAL SODIUM	3313	2206	MILLIGRAMS
TOTAL FIBRE	20	13	GRAMS
% CALORIES FROM FAT	11	9	

CORN BREADS

The three recipes in this section feature the staple grain of the Western Hemisphere: corn. Each of these recipes is a different variation of the use of corn in yeast bread, and you'll find each to be delightful in its own way.

Cornmeal Honey Bread

This simple bread has a white-bread look with a corn-bread crunch.

1½-pound

1½ teaspoons active dry yeast

3 cups bread flour

½ cup cornmeal

1½ teaspoons salt

3 tablespoons honey

1 tablespoon butter

¾ cup warm buttermilk

3 ounces warm water

1-pound

1 teaspoon active dry yeast

2 cups bread flour

⅓ cup cornmeal

1 teaspoon salt

2 tablespoons honey

½ tablespoon butter

½ cup warm buttermilk

¼ cup warm water

Note:

For machines with yeast dispensers, use 3 teaspoons of yeast for the 1½-pound loaf.

NUTRITIONAL ANALYSIS			
	1½-POUND	1-POUND	
TOTAL COLORIES	2084	1371	
TOTAL PROTEIN	63	42	GRAMS
TOTAL CARBOHYDRATES	405	270	GRAMS
TOTAL FAT	22	13	GRAMS
TOTAL SATURATED FAT	9	5	GRAMS
TOTAL CHOLESTEROL	47	26	MILLIGRAMS
TOTAL SODIUM	3345	2230	MILLIGRAMS
TOTAL FIBRE	13	9	GRAMS
% CALORIES FROM FAT	9	8	

Southwestern Pumpkin Bread

Pumpkin, a staple vegetable in Latin America, is good with Mexican food, such as refried beans, or Southwestern fare. Both the pumpkin and the corn give this bread a rich yellow color.

1½-pound

1½ teaspoons active dry yeast

3 cups bread flour

¼ cup cornmeal

1½ teaspoons salt

¼ cup brown sugar

½ cup canned pumpkin

1 egg

5 ounces warm water

1-pound

1 teaspoon active dry yeast

2 cups bread flour

2 tablespoons cornmeal

1 teaspoon salt

2 tablespoons brown sugar

⅓ cup canned pumpkin

1 egg

2½ ounces warm water

Note:

For machines with yeast dispensers, use 3 teaspoons of yeast for the 1½-pound loaf.

NUTRITIONAL ANALYSIS			
	1½-POUND	1-POUND	
TOTAL CALORIES	1920	1252	
TOTAL PROTEIN	60	42	GRAMS
TOTAL CARBOHYDRATES	386	245	GRAMS
TOTAL FAT	13	10	GRAMS
TOTAL SATURATED FAT	3	2	GRAMS
TOTAL CHOLESTEROL	213	213	MILLIGRAMS
TOTAL SODIUM	3296	2214	MILLIGRAMS
TOTAL FIBRE	10	6	GRAMS
% CALORIES FROM FAT	6	7	

White Corn Bread

This crunchy bread has a great look and texture. Try it with soup.

1½-pound

1½ teaspoons active dry yeast

¼ cup brown sugar

2¼ cups + 2 tablespoons bread
flour

2 teaspoons salt

1 cup white cornmeal

2 eggs

2 tablespoons butter

7 ounces warm milk

1-pound

1 teaspoon active dry yeast

3 tablespoons brown sugar

1½ cups + 2 tablespoons bread
flour

1½ teaspoons salt

⅔ cup white cornmeal

1 egg

1½ tablespoons butter

5 ounces warm milk

Notes:

1. For machines with yeast dispensers, use 3 teaspoons of yeast for the 1½-pound loaf.
2. Yellow cornmeal may be substituted for white cornmeal.

NUTRITIONAL ANALYSIS			
	1½-POUND	1-POUND	
TOTAL CALORIES	2519	1549	
TOTAL PROTEIN	78	46	GRAMS
TOTAL CARBOHYDRATES	446	273	GRAMS
TOTAL FAT	46	31	GRAMS
TOTAL SATURATED FAT	20	14	GRAMS
TOTAL CHOLESTEROL	497	266	MILLIGRAMS
TOTAL SODIUM	4566	3385	MILLIGRAMS
TOTAL FIBRE	20	13	GRAMS
% CALORIES FROM FAT	17	18	

OAT BREADS

The breads in this section all include rolled oats in their recipes. Rolled oats (oatmeal) give the bread a soft, spongy texture and good, rich flavor, not to mention additional nutritional benefits. Oatmeal lovers will find that the variety of other ingredients used in the recipes complements the oat flavor and texture, producing some interesting breads.

Nebraska Oatmeal Bread

This traditional oatmeal bread is easy to make, uses basic ingredients, and is tasty and nutritious. The loaf is fairly densely textured.

1½-pound

1½ teaspoons active dry yeast

2½ tablespoons brown sugar

2 cups bread flour

1½ teaspoons salt

1 cup rolled oats

1 tablespoon butter

1 cup warm milk

¼ cup warm water

1-pound

1 teaspoon active dry yeast

1½ tablespoons brown sugar

1⅓ cups bread flour

1 teaspoon salt

⅔ cup rolled oats

1 tablespoon butter

5 ounces warm milk

2 tablespoons warm water

Notes:

1. For machines with yeast dispensers, use 3 teaspoons of yeast for the 1½-pound loaf.
2. For a light-texture loaf, add an extra ½ teaspoon of yeast and an extra tablespoon of warm water for the 1½-pound recipe. Add ¼ teaspoon of yeast and ½ tablespoon of water for the 1-pound loaf.

NUTRITIONAL ANALYSIS			
	1½ -POUND	1-POUND	
TOTAL CALORIES	1641	1114	
TOTAL PROTEIN	55	37	GRAMS
TOTAL CARBOHYDRATES	299	197	GRAMS
TOTAL FAT	24	20	GRAMS
TOTAL SATURATED FAT	10	9	GRAMS
TOTAL CHOLESTEROL	41	37	MILLIGRAMS
TOTAL SODIUM	3341	2222	MILLIGRAMS
TOTAL FIBRE	13	9	GRAMS
% CALORIES FROM FAT	13	16	

Pistachio Oatmeal Bread

The distinctive flavor of pistachio nuts permeates this loaf. To get the best distribution of the pistachio oil in the dough, add the nuts at the beginning rather than at the mix-cycle beep.

1½-pound

1½ teaspoons active dry yeast

¾ cup rolled oats

2½ cups bread flour

1 teaspoon salt

1 teaspoon sugar

1½ tablespoons butter

3 tablespoons honey

¾ cup warm milk

3 ounces warm water

⅓ cup chopped pistachio nuts

1-pound

1 teaspoon active dry yeast

½ cup rolled oats

1⅔ cups bread flour

½ teaspoon salt

½ teaspoon sugar

1 tablespoon butter

2 tablespoons honey

½ cup warm milk

¼ cup warm water

¼ cup chopped pistachio nuts

Note:

For machines with yeast dispensers, use 3 teaspoons of yeast for the 1½-pound loaf.

NUTRITIONAL ANALYSIS			
	1½-POUND	1-POUND	
TOTAL CALORIES	2157	1460	
TOTAL PROTEIN	64	43	GRAMS
TOTAL CARBOHYDRATES	359	239	GRAMS
TOTAL FAT	53	38	GRAMS
TOTAL SATURATED FAT	15	11	GRAMS
TOTAL CHOLESTEROL	54	36	MILLIGRAMS
TOTAL SODIUM	2239	1138	MILLIGRAMS
TOTAL FIBRE	14	9	GRAMS
% CALORIES FROM FAT	22	23	

Soy Oatmeal Bread

The addition of soy flour to this oatmeal bread boosts the nutritional level of the bread, particularly the protein content. This is a good low-fat bread.

1½-pound

1 teaspoon active dry yeast

⅓ cup soy flour

1¾ cups bread flour

1¼ cups rolled oats

½ teaspoon salt

1½ tablespoons butter

5 tablespoons molasses

7 ounces warm water

1-pound

½ teaspoon active dry yeast

¼ cup soy flour

1¼ cups bread flour

¾ cup rolled oats

¼ teaspoon salt

1 tablespoon butter

3 tablespoons molasses

5 ounces warm water

Note:

For machines with yeast dispensers, use 2 teaspoons of yeast for the 1½-pound loaf and 1 teaspoon for the 1-pound loaf.

NUTRITIONAL ANALYSIS			
	1½-POUND	1-POUND	
TOTAL CALORIES	1821	1218	
TOTAL PROTEIN	62	43	GRAMS
TOTAL CARBOHYDRATES	325	217	GRAMS
TOTAL FAT	28	18	GRAMS
TOTAL SATURATED FAT	12	8	GRAMS
TOTAL CHOLESTEROL	47	31	MILLIGRAMS
TOTAL SODIUM	1158	589	MILLIGRAMS
TOTAL FIBRE	16	10	GRAMS
% CALORIES FROM FAT	14	14	

Sunflower Oatmeal Bread

The sunflower seeds secrete an oil that mixes throughout the dough and gives this bread a fine, nutty flavor. It's excellent for breakfast toast.

1½-pound

1½ teaspoons active dry yeast

2¼ cups bread flour

¼ cup sunflower seeds

1 teaspoon salt

¼ cup rolled oats

½ cup whole-wheat flour

½ teaspoon sugar

1 egg

1 tablespoon butter

1 tablespoon molasses

1½ tablespoons honey

3 ounces warm buttermilk

½ cup warm water

1-pound

1 teaspoon active dry yeast

1½ cups bread flour

2 tablespoons sunflower seeds

½ teaspoon salt

2 tablespoons rolled oats

½ cup whole-wheat flour

½ teaspoon sugar

1 egg

1 tablespoon butter

½ tablespoon molasses

1 tablespoon honey

¼ cup warm buttermilk

3 ounces warm water

Notes:

1. For machines with yeast dispensers, use 3 teaspoons of yeast for the 1½-pound loaf.
2. Sunflower seeds may be added at the mix-cycle beep, if your machine is so equipped.

NUTRITIONAL ANALYSIS			
	1½-POUND	1-POUND	
TOTAL CALORIES	1969	1387	
TOTAL PROTEIN	66	48	GRAMS
TOTAL CARBOHYDRATES	336	233	GRAMS
TOTAL FAT	41	30	GRAMS
TOTAL SATURATED FAT	12	11	GRAMS
TOTAL CHOLESTEROL	252	249	MILLIGRAMS
TOTAL SODIUM	2278	1182	MILLIGRAMS
TOTAL FIBRE	15	12	GRAMS
% CALORIES FROM FAT	19	20	

EXOTIC-GRAIN BREADS

This section includes five recipes that make use of unusual bread-making grains. Barley, brown rice, millet, quinoa, and soy are all featured. Each bread has its own unique flavor.

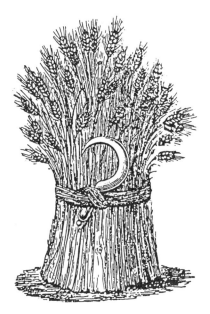

Barley Three-Seed Bread

The combination of barley, poppy seeds, sesame seeds, and sunflower seeds makes this bread unique, both in flavor and texture. It's excellent with salads.

1½-pound

1½ teaspoons active dry yeast

3 tablespoons sugar

2 cups bread flour

1 teaspoon poppy seeds

2 teaspoons sunflower seeds

2 teaspoons sesame seeds

1 tablespoon dough enhancer (optional)

1 cup barley flour

½ teaspoon garlic salt

1 teaspoon salt

1 tablespoon nonfat dry milk

1 cup + 1 tablespoon warm water

1½ tablespoons butter

1-pound

1 teaspoon active dry yeast

2 tablespoons sugar

1⅓ cups bread flour

½ teaspoon poppy seeds

1½ teaspoons sunflower seeds

1½ teaspoons sesame seeds

½ tablespoon dough enhancer (optional)

⅔ cup barley flour

¼ teaspoon garlic salt

½ teaspoon salt

½ tablespoon nonfat dry milk

5½ ounces warm water

1 tablespoon butter

Notes:
1. For machines with yeast dispensers, use 3 teaspoons of yeast for the 1½-pound loaf.
2. This bread is somewhat crumbly. The addition of the dough enhancer, if available, will help the bread stick together, and give it a smoother texture.

NUTRITIONAL ANALYSIS			
	1½-POUND	1-POUND	
TOTAL CALORIES	1790	1192	
TOTAL PROTEIN	53	35	GRAMS
TOTAL CARBOHYDRATES	312	208	GRAMS
TOTAL FAT	31	21	GRAMS
TOTAL SATURATED FAT	12	8	GRAMS
TOTAL CHOLESTEROL	48	32	MILLIGRAMS
TOTAL SODIUM	3240	1622	MILLIGRAMS
TOTAL FIBRE	20	13	GRAMS
% CALORIES FROM FAT	16	16	

Brown-Rice Bread

A soft, moist texture and light brown color characterize this bread. White rice can be substituted for brown rice.

1½-pound

1½ teaspoons active dry yeast

1 teaspoon sugar

3 cups bread flour

1½ teaspoons salt

¾ cup cooked brown rice

1½ tablespoons olive oil

3 tablespoons honey

4½ ounces warm buttermilk

3 ounces warm water

1-pound

1 teaspoon active dry yeast

½ teaspoon sugar

2 cups bread flour

1 teaspoon salt

½ cup cooked brown rice

1 tablespoon olive oil

2 tablespoons honey

3 ounces warm buttermilk

¼ cup warm water

Note:

For machines with yeast dispensers, use 3 teaspoons of yeast for the 1½-pound loaf.

NUTRITIONAL ANALYSIS			
	1½-POUND	1-POUND	
TOTAL CALORIES	2098	1396	
TOTAL PROTEIN	60	40	GRAMS
TOTAL CARBOHYDRATES	394	262	GRAMS
TOTAL FAT	29	20	GRAMS
TOTAL SATURATED FAT	4	3	GRAMS
TOTAL CHOLESTEROL	12	8	MILLIGRAMS
TOTAL SODIUM	3295	2197	MILLIGRAMS
TOTAL FIBRE	7	5	GRAMS
% CALORIES FROM FAT	13	13	

Millet Bread

Millet is a small, round, hard grain that requires soaking before use. It is also available in ground form as millet flour. The texture of this bread is crunchy, though also light due to the mixture of whole-wheat and bread flours.

1½-pound

1½ teaspoons active dry yeast

1 cup whole-wheat flour

2 cups bread flour

1 teaspoon salt

1 cup warm water

½ cup raw millet (or millet cereal)

2 tablespoons olive oil

3 tablespoons honey

1 egg

1-pound

1 teaspoon active dry yeast

⅔ cup whole-wheat flour

1½ cups bread flour

½ teaspoon salt

⅔ cup warm water

⅓ cup raw millet (or millet cereal)

1½ tablespoons olive oil

2 tablespoons honey

1 egg

Notes:

1. For machines with yeast dispensers, use 3 teaspoons of yeast for the 1½-pound loaf.
2. Soak the millet in the warm water for 45–60 minutes before adding the grain and the water to the recipe.

NUTRITIONAL ANALYSIS			
	1½-POUND	1-POUND	
TOTAL CALORIES	2279	1645	
TOTAL PROTEIN	68	50	GRAMS
TOTAL CARBOHYDRATES	409	289	GRAMS
TOTAL FAT	43	33	GRAMS
TOTAL SATURATED FAT	7	5	GRAMS
TOTAL CHOLESTEROL	213	213	MILLIGRAMS
TOTAL SODIUM	2207	1137	MILLIGRAMS
TOTAL FIBRE	21	14	GRAMS
% CALORIES FROM FAT	17	18	

Sesame Quinoa Bread

Quinoa, native to South America, is one of the grains highest in protein. Since it contains no gluten, it must be combined with wheat flour. Sesame Quinoa Bread has a nutty, earthy flavor, making it an excellent sandwich bread.

1½-pound

1½ teaspoons active dry yeast

3 tablespoons sugar

2 cups bread flour

½ cup quinoa flour

3 tablespoons sesame seeds

½ teaspoon oregano

½ teaspoon ground caraway seeds

½ cup whole-wheat flour

1½ teaspoons salt

1½ tablespoons nonfat dry milk

9 ounces warm water

2 tablespoons butter

1-pound

1 teaspoon active dry yeast

2 tablespoons sugar

1⅓ cups bread flour

⅓ cup quinoa flour

2 tablespoons sesame seeds

¼ teaspoon oregano

¼ teaspoon ground caraway seeds

⅓ cup whole-wheat flour

1 teaspoon salt

1 tablespoon nonfat dry milk

¾ cup warm water

1½ tablespoons butter

Note:

For machines with yeast dispensers, use 3 teaspoons of yeast for the 1½-pound loaf.

NUTRITIONAL ANALYSIS			
	1½-POUND	1-POUND	
TOTAL CALORIES	2053	1379	
TOTAL PROTEIN	62	41	GRAMS
TOTAL CARBOHYDRATES	350	232	GRAMS
TOTAL FAT	47	33	GRAMS
TOTAL SATURATED FAT	17	13	GRAMS
TOTAL CHOLESTEROL	64	48	MILLIGRAMS
TOTAL SODIUM	3256	2171	MILLIGRAMS
TOTAL FIBRE	14	9	GRAMS
% CALORIES FROM FAT	21	22	

Soy Bread

This white bread is enriched by the addition of high-protein soy flour.

1½-pound

1½ teaspoons active dry yeast

1½ tablespoons sugar

½ cup soy flour

2½ cups bread flour

1½ teaspoons salt

9 ounces warm milk

1½ tablespoons butter

1-pound

1 teaspoon active dry yeast

1 tablespoon sugar

⅓ cup soy flour

1⅔ cups bread flour

1 teaspoon salt

¾ cup warm milk

1 tablespoon butter

Note:

For machines with yeast dispensers, use 3 teaspoons of yeast for the 1½-pound loaf.

NUTRITIONAL ANALYSIS			
	1½-POUND	1-POUND	
TOTAL CALORIES	1746	1165	
TOTAL PROTEIN	75	50	GRAMS
TOTAL CARBOHYDRATES	300	200	GRAMS
TOTAL FAT	27	18	GRAMS
TOTAL SATURATED FAT	13	9	GRAMS
TOTAL CHOLESTEROL	58	39	MILLIGRAMS
TOTAL SODIUM	3355	2236	MILLIGRAMS
TOTAL FIBRE	8	5	GRAMS
% CALORIES FROM FAT	14	14	

MULTIPLE-GRAIN BREADS

This section features seven mixed-grain breads in which the taste of grain dominates. These unique combinations of grains are especially designed for whole-grain-bread lovers.

Bran & Rye Bread

This light wheat-rye bread has added oat bran for texture, flavor, and nutrients. It has a light wheat taste and texture.

1½-pound

1½ teaspoons active dry yeast

2½ tablespoons brown sugar

1 cup + 1½ tablespoons bread flour

½ cup whole-wheat flour

¾ cup rye flour

¾ cup oat bran

2 teaspoons salt

2 tablespoons butter

9 ounces warm buttermilk

1-pound

1 teaspoon active dry yeast

1½ tablespoons brown sugar

⅔ cup + 1 tablespoon bread flour

⅓ cup whole-wheat flour

½ cup rye flour

½ cup oat bran

1½ teaspoons salt

1½ tablespoons butter

¾ cup warm buttermilk

Notes:

1. For machines with yeast dispensers, use 3 teaspoons of yeast for the 1½-pound loaf.
2. If your machine is equipped with a whole-grain cycle, use it for this bread.

NUTRITIONAL ANALYSIS			
	1½-POUND	1-POUND	
TOTAL CALORIES	1691	1130	
TOTAL PROTEIN	60	40	GRAMS
TOTAL CARBOHYDRATES	300	197	GRAMS
TOTAL FAT	35	25	GRAMS
TOTAL SATURATED FAT	17	12	GRAMS
TOTAL CHOLESTEROL	85	62	MILLIGRAMS
TOTAL SODIUM	4460	3328	MILLIGRAMS
TOTAL FIBRE	31	21	GRAMS
% CALORIES FROM FAT	18	20	

Corn, Wheat, & Rye Bread

This is a very crunchy whole-grain bread with a good wheat flavor and a hint of rye.

1½-pound

2 teaspoons active dry yeast

3 tablespoons brown sugar

½ cup cornmeal

1¼ cups whole-wheat flour

1¼ cups rye flour

1½ teaspoons salt

3 tablespoons butter

9 ounces warm water

1-pound

1½ teaspoons active dry yeast

2 tablespoons brown sugar

¼ cup + 2 tablespoons cornmeal

1 cup whole-wheat flour

¾ cup rye flour

1 teaspoon salt

2 tablespoons butter

¾ cup warm water

Notes:

1. For machines with yeast dispensers, use 4 teaspoons of yeast for the 1½-pound loaf.
2. If your machine is equipped with a whole-grain cycle, use it for this bread.

	NUTRITIONAL ANALYSIS		
	1½-POUND	1-POUND	
TOTAL CALORIES	1648	1158	
TOTAL PROTEIN	40	29	GRAMS
TOTAL CARBOHYDRATES	296	210	GRAMS
TOTAL FAT	42	28	GRAMS
TOTAL SATURATED FAT	22	15	GRAMS
TOTAL CHOLESTEROL	93	62	MILLIGRAMS
TOTAL SODIUM	3242	2164	MILLIGRAMS
TOTAL FIBRE	45	32	GRAMS
% CALORIES FROM FAT	230	22	

Mixed-Grain Bread

This bread combines many different grains for a full-grain taste. It doesn't rise much, due to the low-gluten content of the ingredients, but it is a wonderful, healthful bread with an earthy aroma.

1½-pound

2½ teaspoons active dry yeast

⅔ cup bread flour

½ teaspoon caraway seeds

2 teaspoons salt

½ cup rice flour

⅔ cup buckwheat flour

⅔ cup oat flour

⅔ cup rye flour

5 tablespoons molasses

1 egg

7 ounces warm water

3 tablespoons raisins

2 tablespoons gluten powder (optional)

1-pound

1½ teaspoons active dry yeast

½ cup bread flour

½ teaspoon caraway seeds

1½ teaspoons salt

⅓ cup rice flour

½ cup buckwheat flour

½ cup oat flour

½ cup rye flour

4 tablespoons molasses

1 egg

4½ ounces warm water

2 tablespoons raisins

1½ tablespoons gluten powder (optional)

Notes:

1. For machines with yeast dispensers, use 4½ teaspoons of yeast for the 1½-pound loaf.
2. If your machine is equipped with a whole-grain cycle, use it for this bread.
3. Raisins may be added at the mix-cycle beep, if your machine is so equipped.

NUTRITIONAL ANALYSIS			
	1½-POUND	1-POUND	
TOTAL CALORIES	1877	1403	
TOTAL PROTEIN	52	39	GRAMS
TOTAL CARBOHYDRATES	392	289	GRAMS
TOTAL FAT	13	11	GRAMS
TOTAL SATURATED FAT	3	2	GRAMS
TOTAL CHOLESTEROL	213	213	MILLIGRAMS
TOTAL SODIUM	4414	3329	MILLIGRAMS
TOTAL FIBRE	27	20	GRAMS
% CALORIES FROM FAT	6	7	

Oat, Rice & Rye Bread

This bread doesn't rise much, but with its tight texture and flat top, it tastes delicious.

1½-pound

2 teaspoons active dry yeast

1½ tablespoons gluten powder

¾ cup bread flour

1 teaspoon ground caraway seeds

¾ cup rice flour

¾ cup oat flour

¾ cup rye flour

1½ teaspoons salt

2 tablespoons brown sugar

2 tablespoons butter

9 ounces warm water

1-pound

1½ teaspoons active dry yeast

1 tablespoon gluten powder

½ cup bread flour

½ teaspoon ground caraway seeds

½ cup rice flour

½ cup oat flour

½ cup rye flour

1 teaspoon salt

1½ tablespoons brown sugar

1½ tablespoons butter

¾ ounces warm water

Notes:

1. For machines with yeast dispensers, use 4 teaspoons of yeast for the 1½-pound loaf.
2. If your machine is equipped with a whole-grain cycle, use it for this bread.
3. For a slightly higher rise, try adding an extra ½ teaspoon of yeast.

NUTRITIONAL ANALYSIS			
	1½-POUND	1-POUND	
TOTAL CALORIES	1774	1208	
TOTAL PROTEIN	51	34	GRAMS
TOTAL CARBOHYDRATES	330	222	GRAMS
TOTAL FAT	30	22	GRAMS
TOTAL SATURATED FAT	15	11	GRAMS
TOTAL CHOLESTEROL	62	47	MILLIGRAMS
TOTAL SODIUM	3217	2146	MILLIGRAMS
TOTAL FIBRE	30	20	GRAMS
% CALORIES FROM FAT	15	16	

Whole-Wheat & Rice Bread

This bread uses only wheat and rice flours, so the result is a bread similar to 100 percent–wheat bread, both in texture and flavor. The rice flour has a smoothing effect on the texture, but it contains no gluten, so the loaf will rise slightly less than a normal 100 percent–wheat loaf.

1½-pound

2 teaspoons active dry yeast

2¼ cups whole-wheat flour

½ teaspoon mace

¾ cup rice flour

2 teaspoons salt

2 tablespoons butter

3 tablespoons honey

1 cup warm water

¼ cup raisins

1-pound

1½ teaspoons active dry yeast

1½ cups whole-wheat flour

¼ teaspoon mace

½ cup rice flour

1½ teaspoons salt

1½ tablespoons butter

2 tablespoons honey

5½ ounces warm water

3 tablespoons raisins

Notes:

1. For machines with yeast dispensers, use 4 teaspoons of yeast for the 1½-pound loaf.
2. If your machine is equipped with a whole-grain cycle, use it for this bread.
3. Raisins may be added at the mix-cycle beep, if your machine is so equipped.
4. For machines with low-power motors, add 2 tablespoons of warm water for the 1½-pound loaf.

NUTRITIONAL ANALYSIS			
	1½-POUND	1-POUND	
TOTAL CALORIES	1852	1289	
TOTAL PROTEIN	47	32	GRAMS
TOTAL CARBOHYDRATES	369	256	GRAMS
TOTAL FAT	30	22	GRAMS
TOTAL SATURATED FAT	16	12	GRAMS
TOTAL CHOLESTEROL	62	47	MILLIGRAMS
TOTAL SODIUM	4276	3208	MILLIGRAMS
TOTAL FIBRE	40	27	GRAMS
% CALORIES FROM FAT	14	15	

Whole-Wheat, Bran & Oat Bread

This bread has a soft texture and a mild wheat-oat flavor. Because bread flour comprises half the flour, it rises well and yields a nice-looking, good-tasting loaf.

1½-pound

2 teaspoons active dry yeast

3 tablespoons brown sugar

1½ tablespoons gluten powder

1½ cups bread flour

⅓ cup oat bran

¾ cup oat flour

¾ cup whole-wheat flour

2 teaspoons salt

3½ tablespoons butter

1¼ cups warm water

1-pound

1½ teaspoons active dry yeast

2 tablespoons brown sugar

1 tablespoon gluten powder

1 cup bread flour

¼ cup oat bran

½ cup oat flour

½ cup whole-wheat flour

1½ teaspoons salt

2½ tablespoons butter

6½ ounces warm water

Note:

For machines with yeast dispensers, use 3½ teaspoons of yeast for the 1½-pound loaf.

NUTRITIONAL ANALYSIS			
	1½-POUND	1-POUND	
TOTAL CALORIES	2031	1406	
TOTAL PROTEIN	67	45	GRAMS
TOTAL CARBOHYDRATES	344	238	GRAMS
TOTAL FAT	50	35	GRAMS
TOTAL SATURATED FAT	26	18	GRAMS
TOTAL CHOLESTEROL	109	78	MILLIGRAMS
TOTAL SODIUM	4289	3217	MILLIGRAMS
TOTAL FIBRE	32	22	GRAMS
% CALORIES FROM FAT	22	22	

Whole-Wheat, Rye & Oat Bread

A good dense texture and hearty flavor characterize this bread. It's excellent eaten warm or toasted, and it's especially good with all kinds of cheese.

1½-pound

2 teaspoons active dry yeast

¾ cup oat flour

¾ cup rye flour

1½ cups whole-wheat flour

1½ teaspoons salt

3 tablespoons butter

3 tablespoons honey

1 cup + 1 tablespoon warm water

1-pound

1½ teaspoons active dry yeast

½ cup oat flour

½ cup rye flour

1 cup whole-wheat flour

1 teaspoon salt

2 tablespoons butter

2 tablespoons honey

5½ ounces warm water

Notes:

1. For machines with yeast dispensers, use 4 teaspoons of yeast for the 1½-pound loaf.
2. If your machine is equipped with a whole-grain cycle, use it for this bread.

NUTRITIONAL ANALYSIS			
	1½-POUND	1-POUND	
TOTAL CALORIES	1675	1118	
TOTAL PROTEIN	45	30	GRAMS
TOTAL CARBOHYDRATES	304	203	GRAMS
TOTAL FAT	41	27	GRAMS
TOTAL SATURATED FAT	22	15	GRAMS
TOTAL CHOLESTEROL	93	62	MILLIGRAMS
TOTAL SODIUM	3209	2139	MILLIGRAMS
TOTAL FIBRE	47	31	GRAMS
% CALORIES FROM FAT	22	22	

SPONGE BREADS

These breads all require some advance preparation. They use a "sponge," a yeast mixture made in advance and allowed to proof over a period of time. The sponge is then added to the remaining ingredients in the bread machine. Sponge breads tend to be lighter in texture than their "non-sponge" counterparts, since the yeast has more time to work on the mixture.

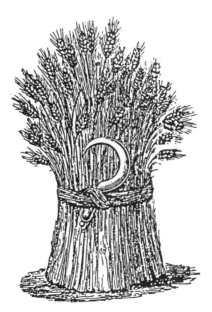

Neapolitan Whole-Wheat Bread

This bread is similar to French bread, with a light whole-wheat flavor and texture. It's excellent eaten fresh and warm.

1½-pound

SPONGE:

1 teaspoon active dry yeast

1 cup bread flour

¾ cup whole-wheat flour

1 teaspoon sugar

8½ ounces warm water

REMAINING INGREDIENTS:

1¼ cup bread flour

1½ teaspoons salt

2½ ounces warm water

1-pound

SPONGE:

½ teaspoon active dry yeast

¾ cup bread flour

½ cup whole-wheat flour

1 teaspoon sugar

5½ ounces warm water

REMAINING INGREDIENTS:

¾ cup bread flour

1 teaspoon salt

3 tablespoons warm water

Instructions:

1. Prepare sponge. Place the warm water in a large (3-quart) bowl, and then sprinkle sugar and yeast over the water and stir until dissolved. Let the yeast proof for about 10 minutes (bubbles and froth will appear), and then add the flour.
2. Mix until smooth and cover with plastic wrap.
3. Let the sponge sit for at least 4 hours at room temperature. After that, the sponge may be refrigerated for up to a week if it won't be used immediately. If refrigerated, however, it must be brought back to room temperature before being used.
4. Place sponge in bread machine and add remaining ingredients.

NUTRITIONAL ANALYSIS			
	1½-POUND	1-POUND	
TOTAL CALORIES	1441	965	
TOTAL PROTEIN	50	33	GRAMS
TOTAL CARBOHYDRATES	294	197	GRAMS
TOTAL FAT	7	5	GRAMS
TOTAL SATURATED FAT	1	1	GRAMS
TOTAL CHOLESTEROL	0	0	
TOTAL SODIUM	3205	2136	MILLIGRAMS
TOTAL FIBRE	16	11	GRAMS
% CALORIES FROM FAT	4	4	

Semolina Bread

Pasta flour (semolina), the main ingredient in this bread, gives a smooth texture and a wonderful taste and appearance.

1½ -pound

SPONGE:

1½ teaspoons activedry yeast

1 cup semolina flour

1 cup warm water

REMAINING INGREDIENTS:

1 large red bell pepper, chopped

1½ teaspoons salt

2 cups bread flour

2 tablespoons olive oil

1-pound

SPONGE:

1 teaspoon active dry yeast

⅔ cup semolina flour

⅔ cup warm water

REMAINING INGREDIENTS:

⅔ large red bell pepper, chopped

1 teaspoon salt

1⅓ cups bread flour

1½ tablespoons olive oil

Instructions:

1. Prepare sponge. Place warm water in a 3-quart bowl. Sprinkle the yeast on the water and gently stir. Then add the flour and mix.
2. Cover the mixture with plastic wrap and let it sit at least 1 hour, stirring occasionally.
3. Place sponge and remaining ingredients in the bread machine.

NUTRITIONAL ANALYSIS			
	1½-POUND	1-POUND	
TOTAL CALORIES	1642	1114	
TOTAL PROTEIN	48	32	GRAMS
TOTAL CARBOHYDRATES	280	187	GRAMS
TOTAL FAT	33	24	GRAMS
TOTAL SATURATED FAT	4	3	GRAMS
TOTAL CHOLESTEROL	0	0	
TOTAL SODIUM	3205	2137	MILLIGRAMS
TOTAL FIBRE	7	5	GRAMS
% CALORIES FROM FAT	18	20	

Whole-Wheat Country Rye Bread

1½-pound

SPONGE:

2 teaspoons active dry yeast

½ cup rye flour

½ cup whole-wheat flour

1½ tablespoons molasses

1½ tablespoons honey

1 cup warm water

REMAINING INGREDIENTS:

1½ cups bread flour

2 tablespoons rolled oats

2 tablespoons buckwheat flour

2 tablespoons oat bran

1 teaspoon salt

1½ tablespoons olive oil

1-pound

SPONGE:

1½ teaspoons active dry yeast

⅓ cup rye flour

⅓ cup whole-wheat flour

1 tablespoon molasses

1 tablespoon honey

5½ ounces warm water

REMAINING INGREDIENTS:

1 cup bread flour

1½ tablespoons rolled oats

2 tablespoons buckwheat flour

2 tablespoons oat bran

½ teaspoon salt

1 tablespoon olive oil

Instructions:

1. Prepare sponge. Pour the warm water and honey into a 2- or 3-quart bowl. Add the yeast and let it proof for 10 minutes (until bubbly and frothy).
2. Add molasses, whole-wheat flour, and rye flour, and mix together. Cover with a cloth or plastic wrap, and let the sponge sit for at least 1 hour.
3. Place the sponge in the bread machine with the remaining ingredients.

NUTRITIONAL ANALYSIS			
	1½-POUND	1-POUND	
TOTAL CALORIES	1623	1112	
TOTAL PROTEIN	45	32	GRAMS
TOTAL CARBOHYDRATES	303	207	GRAMS
TOTAL FAT	28	19	GRAMS
TOTAL SATURATED FAT	4	3	GRAMS
TOTAL CHOLESTEROL	0	0	
TOTAL SODIUM	2163	1087	MILLIGRAMS
TOTAL FIBRE	21	15	GRAMS
% CALORIES FROM FAT	15	15	

APPENDIXES

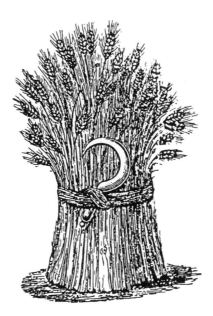

Nutritional Quick Reference

All the recipes in this book were analyzed for nutritional value. The following lists contain the top 10 breads in each category, in order.

Highest-Fibre Breads
- Whole-Wheat Cranberry Bread
- Whole-Wheat Egg Bread
- Whole-Wheat Sally Lunn Bread
- Corn, Wheat & Rye Bread
- Date Molasses Bread
- Whole-Wheat, Rye & Oat Bread
- Whole-Wheat & Rice Bread
- Whole-Wheat Potato Bread
- Buckwheat Rye Bread
- Whole-Wheat Buttermilk Raisin Bread

Lowest-Fat-Content Breads
- Neapolitan Whole-Wheat Bread
- Whole-Wheat Sourdough Bread
- Southwestern Pumpkin Bread
- Mixed-Grain Bread
- Babovka
- Date Molasses Bread
- Swedish Rye Bread
- Cornmeal Honey Bread
- Buttermilk Potato Bread
- Raisin Walnut Bread

Lowest-Calorie Breads
- Neapolitan Whole-Wheat Bread
- Buckwheat Rye Bread
- Oat Rye Bread
- Whole-Wheat Country Rye Bread
- Nebraska Oatmeal Bread
- Semolina Bread
- Whole-Wheat Rye & Oat Bread
- Whole-Wheat & Buckwheat Bread
- Bran & Rye Bread
- Raisin Walnut Bread

Lowest-Sodium Breads
- Dill Rye Bread
- Nut Bread

- Soy Oatmeal Bread
- Shredded-Wheat Nut Bread
- Babovka
- Whole-Wheat Sourdough Bread
- Raisin Walnut Bread
- Whole-Wheat Country Rye Bread
- Buckwheat Rye Bread
- Cashew Date Bread

Overall Healthiest Breads

The following 10 breads are low in calories, sodium, and fat and high in fibre.

- Date Molasses Bread
- Whole-Wheat Sourdough Bread
- Buckwheat Rye Bread
- Dill Rye Bread
- Farmer's Bread
- Oat Rye Bread
- Raisin Walnut Bread
- Whole-Wheat Cranberry Bread
- Neapolitan Whole-Wheat Bread
- Babovka

Measures

Liquid Measure Equivalencies

To ➡ From	teaspoon	tablespoon	ounce	cup	pint
teaspoon	1	3	6	48	96
tablespoon	1/3	1	2	16	32
ounce	1/6	1/2	1	8	16
cup	1/48	1/16	1/8	1	2
pint	1/96	1/48	1/16	1/2	1

Dry Measure Equivalencies

To ➡ From	teaspoon	tablespoon	cup	pint
teaspoon	1	3	48	96
tablespoon	1/3	1	16	32
cup	1/48	1/16	1	2
pint	1/96	1/48	1/2	1

Bread Machine Information

Use the blanks to enter specific information about your bread machine and then use the chart for handy reference.

- ☐ Machine Brand _____
- ☐ Model Number _____
- ☐ Capacity (1 or 1½ pounds) _____
- ☐ Basic White-Bread Recipe:
  - ☐ ☐ Bread Flour _____
  - ☐ ☐ Ounces of Liquid _____
  - ☐ ☐ Liquidity Ratio _____

Index

About the Author

Norman A. Garrett is a college professor and an expert in computers and technology. He received his bachelor's degree from Brigham Young University and his master's and doctoral degrees from Arizona State University. He enjoys cooking and baking, particularly outdoor cooking with old-fashioned Dutch ovens. He lives in rural Illinois with his wife, Margie, and their five children.